VISUAL ILLUSION

QUILTS

Full-Size Templates for 12 Patchwork Projects

by
PAT GASKA

D1536159

DOVER PUBLICATIONS, INC.
New York

A special note of thanks to my family, who has always given me the space to pursue my interests; my friends, who encouraged me to write this book; and my many students, who have grown with me in our knowledge of and appreciation for quiltmaking!

Copyright © 1990 by Pat Gaska.
All rights reserved under Pan American and International Copyright Conventions.

Published in Canada by General Publishing Company, Ltd., 30 Lesmill Road, Don Mills, Toronto, Ontario.
Published in the United Kingdom by Constable and Company, Ltd.

Visual Illusion Quilts: Full-Size Templates for 12 Patchwork Projects is a new work, first published by Dover Publications, Inc., in 1990.

Manufactured in the United States of America
Dover Publications, Inc., 31 East 2nd Street, Mineola, N.Y. 11501

Library of Congress Cataloging-in-Publication Data

Gaska, Pat.
    Visual illusion quilts : full-size templates for 12 patchwork projects /   by Pat Gaska.
        p.   cm.
    ISBN 0-486-26159-X
    1. Patchwork—Patterns. 2. Quilting—Patterns. I. Title.
TT835.G37   1990
746.9′7041—dc20   90-33547
                                                                          CIP

INTRODUCTION

The seed for this book was probably planted twenty years ago when, as an art student, I did two paintings with chevron backgrounds. Those backgrounds created an effect much like a multifold screen that appeared to stand out from the surface of the canvas. Many years later, I incorporated the same chevron design into a quilt. The texture of hand-quilting added an interesting element not found in the paintings, and increased the illusion of depth.

Since then, I've explored more possibilities for achieving the illusion of depth within a quilt's two dimensions, height and width. The variations appear to be endless! There are, of course, other contemporary quilters who work with the same concept, though in styles much different from mine.

All of us, though, must acknowledge that we are building on a tradition, especially noting the Tumbling Blocks and Log Cabin patterns that are a part of our rich heritage as American quilters.

My approach to three-dimensional illusions in quiltmaking is based on a simple idea, and some of the designs in this book are quite simple. The three-dimensional impact becomes apparent when the individual blocks are repeated many times and when the quilts are seen from a distance.

In addition to explaining three-dimensional techniques in quilting, this book offers full-size templates and instructions for twelve wall quilts. My hope is that the reader will begin with these projects and then use them as a springboard for the exploration of many more possibilities.

GENERAL INSTRUCTIONS

DESIGNING THE QUILT

Four basic equilateral shapes are the basis for the quilt blocks in this book—triangle, hexagon, diamond and square. Each block was designed in a similar manner. An equilateral shape is drawn *(Fig. 1)*.

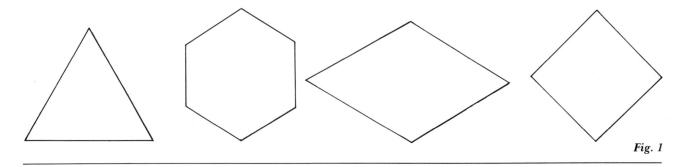

Fig. 1

The shapes are divided into smaller sections, often from the center point out *(Fig. 2)*.

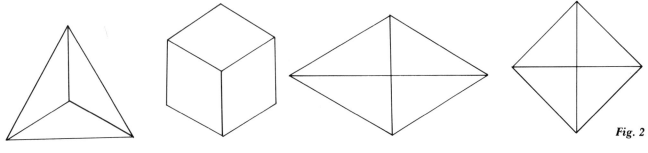

Fig. 2

3

A light source is determined. This source could come from upper or lower left or right. One section remains the lightest, the section opposite is darkest, the other section or sections are medium shades *(Fig. 3)*. I find it helpful to do this shading with a no. 2 lead pencil rather than colored pencils, since the distraction of color is undesirable at this point.

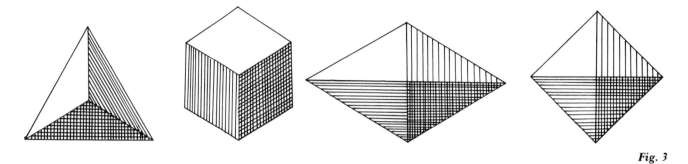

Fig. 3

Numbering the sections helps keep track of which fabric belongs where *(Fig. 4)*.

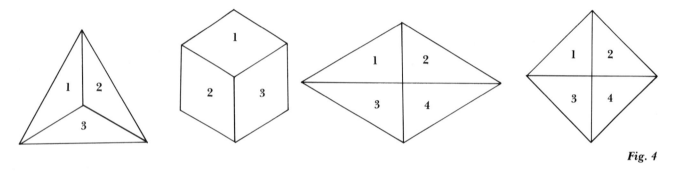

Fig. 4

A number of blocks are then drawn side by side and shaded in *(Fig. 5)*.

Reproducible grids are printed on pages 12–14 for your experimentation.

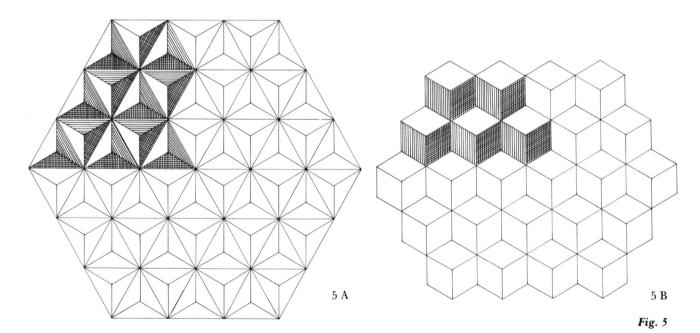

5 A

5 B

Fig. 5

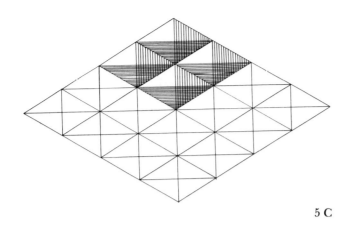

5 C

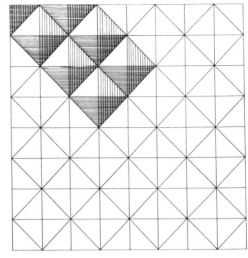

5 D

Fig. 5

Variations

Many variations on this basic technique are possible:

• Off-center division point *(Fig. 6)*

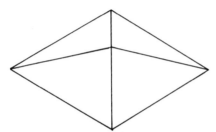

Fig. 6

• Strip-piecing in one or more sections *(Fig. 7)*

• A center shape added *(Fig. 8)*

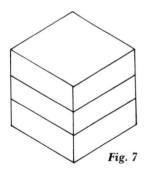

Fig. 7   Fig. 8

• Alternating plain and patterned blocks *(Fig. 9)*

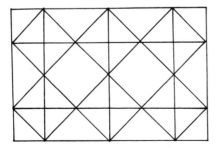

Fig. 9

• Shapes overlapping other shapes *(Fig. 10)*

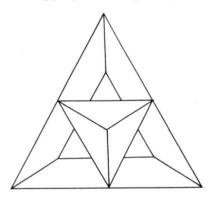

Fig. 10

• Blocks within blocks *(Fig. 11)*

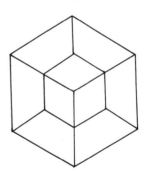

Fig. 11

• Focal points created by color usage, plain areas or shading variations *(Fig. 12)*

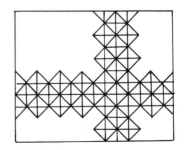

Fig. 12

5

The whole quilt might be planned in detail at this point, with size and borders as considerations, or you may prefer to just let the quilt grow, adding blocks and planning as you go. Either method can work successfully.

Planning the border

A border acts as a frame for the quilt, complementing the overall quilt design. There are many possible approaches:

- A wide band of fabric that provides a needed "resting place" for the eye
- A corner block within the wide border, repeating a design element of the quilt block
- No border—just binding
- A design element of the quilt block encircling the whole quilt
- A series of strips in varying widths
- A wide fragmented patchwork border

Experiment! Don't be afraid to discard a border that doesn't work just because you've invested time and effort in it. In the end, you'll be happier with the results if you start anew.

FABRICS

Preparation

Firmly woven, lightweight, all-cotton fabrics are the best choice for this type of quilt. All fabrics should be pre-washed and, if the piece is to be machine-dried later, also machine-dried now. If the fabrics are going to shrink, it is much better for them to do so now, rather than after the quilt has been sewn together. Pre-washing also removes sizing, making the fabrics softer. Dark colors may need to be washed a second or third time to remove excess dyes.

Choice and placement

Perhaps the most critical step in a successful three-dimensional quilt is fabric choice and placement. Fabrics need to be seen as shades of gray, ranging from light to dark. Particular hues, tones or prints are of secondary importance. Whether the quilt has three sections or 30, a smooth gradation from light to dark is needed (*Fig. 13*). Uneven changes in shading, or gradations that are too similar to one another, should be avoided (*Fig. 14*).

While a single block from the group of fabrics in *Fig. 14* might be pleasing by itself, when many blocks are joined the three-dimensional effect will be weak.

One of several approaches to fabric selection might be taken:

Limited choice. A particular number of fabrics can be used in a consistent way in all the blocks; in other

Fig. 13

Fig. 14

words, each block will be identical to all other blocks. Light, medium, dark shades of a *particular* color can be chosen, light, medium, dark shades of *different* colors can be chosen, or several different prints or a combination of prints and solids can be chosen.

"Scrap" fabrics—unlimited choice. A large number of fabrics should be sorted into light, medium and dark piles. Those lights, mediums and darks will be used in a consistent way in each block.

"True" scrap quilts eliminate *no* color or print, but in the interest of achieving the three-dimensional illusion, some control may be advisable. Large, splashy prints can add interest, but may be distracting. Subtler prints may be the better choice, as they seem to work together well and don't call attention to themselves. It is also possible to control color, sticking perhaps to combinations like green/blue/gray or gold/rust/brown. Remember, the fabrics should be seen as shades of gray—light to dark.

To group fabrics, divide them into the needed number of piles, overlapping them so that a little of each can be seen. Step back several feet from the fabrics and either squint at them or look at them through a colored plastic paddle (available at some toy stores). The paddle (red works well) will "even out" the colors and make a much lighter or darker print obvious. Those fabrics can then be repositioned in another pile

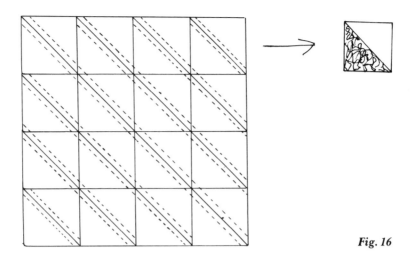

Fig. 15

Fig. 16

or discarded altogether. Chances are, if you are making a true scrap quilt (from fabrics on hand rather than from specially purchased fabrics), you will have many more of one gradation than others. More fabrics may then need to be purchased to round out the selection. A range of eight to ten fabrics in each gradation is sufficient for most projects, but certainly the more the better.

Each time the fabrics are put away, slip each pile into a separate plastic bag, to avoid having to re-sort later.

CONSTRUCTION

Hand or machine-piecing can be used for any of the quilts in this book; however, one method is often preferable to the other. Quick cutting and piecing techniques are possible for some designs.

All templates, except the curved pieces for Peach Pie, include ¼″ seam allowances. Carefully cut out the cardboard templates, *including* the ¼″ seam allowances if machine-piecing, *excluding* the seam allowance if hand-piecing. On machine templates, a small hole can be punched at the intersection of stitching lines. When marking fabrics, a mark can be made at these points and, when piecing, a pin can be placed through the points of pieces to be joined for greater accuracy.

Note that the straight of grain is marked on each template by an arrow.

To make the templates more permanent, glue them to another piece of cardboard before cutting them out, or trace them onto translucent plastic.

Lay the templates on the reverse side of the fabrics, having the arrows parallel to the threads of the fabric. Do not include the selvage edges of the fabrics within the patchwork sections. Draw around the template with a sharp no. 2 pencil. If machine-piecing, also mark the corner dot. If a no. 2 pencil doesn't show up on a particular fabric, use a soft drawing pencil (6B) or a white or silver pencil. Whatever the marking tool, it must be sharp so that pieces are accurately drawn.

For machine-piecing, the line drawn is the *cutting line,* so templates can be laid side-by-side on the fabric to avoid wasting fabric and to save cutting time.

For hand-piecing, the line drawn is the *seam line,* so seam allowances must be added. Place templates ½″ apart and, when cutting, cut in between the pencil lines. Don't be concerned if the allowances are not exactly ¼″; when sewing, you will match seam lines, not the edges of the fabric.

Quick-cutting and sewing techniques for machine-piecing

A lot of time can be saved and better accuracy achieved by using a rotary cutter, mat and cutting guide, available at most fabric and quilt stores. There are a number of excellent books that describe quick cutting and sewing techniques in detail; some basic methods are explained here.

Most templates are marked with a width measurement, running with the straight of grain. To save time, fold or layer fabrics so that it is possible to cut through several layers at a time. Line up the straight of grain of all layers as closely as possible. Cut strips of fabric the width of the template, then mark and cut individual pieces *(Fig. 15).*

For right-angle triangles, layer the two needed fabrics with the right sides together. Mark squares first, drawing alongside the cutting guide, then mark diagonal lines through the center of each square. Place a pin in the center of each triangle, then cut around the whole marked area.

Triangles that form half a square. Machine-stitch ¼″ away on each side of each diagonal line, sewing through the corners of adjacent triangles *(Fig. 16).*

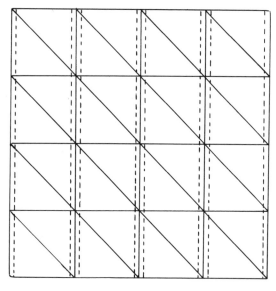

Fig. 17

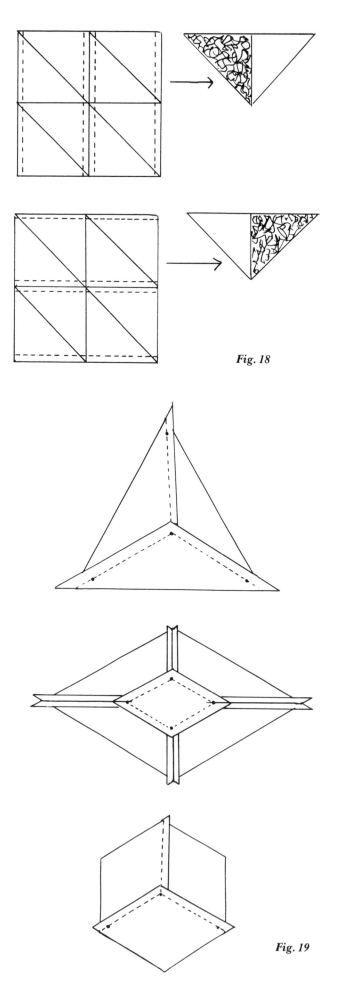

Fig. 18

Fig. 19

Since only a few stitches will be in these corners, they will pull out easily. The time saved by not stopping to raise and lower the presser foot to avoid sewing through the corners will be considerable.

Triangles that form half a triangle. Mark as above, but sew along the short sides of the triangle, rather than along diagonals *(Fig. 17).*

Note! Check your quilt block! Triangles fit into a larger triangle in a particular way. It will make a difference whether the seam runs along one side of the triangle or the other—two different results are possible *(Fig. 18).*

Now return the section to the cutting board and, using the rotary cutter, cut out the triangles on the marked lines and press the seams to one side.

Quick techniques are wonderful, but it is easy to get carried away and find that sections are joined incorrectly or that you have far more of a particular unit than needed.

Think before you cut and sew! Haste makes waste!

Traditional piecing methods

Piece carefully! Most designs have at least one template with a very sharp 30° or 60° angle that will require extra care to piece accurately. Better results may be achieved in some instances by ironing seams open, rather than to one side.

When a number of points meet at the same place, as in Parquet Stars, Night Window or Blue Star, excess fabric should be trimmed from the seam allowances near the point.

Even if the quilt is machine-pieced, problem areas where a number of points meet can be hand-pieced. Machine-piece to within an inch or so of the point, then complete the seam by hand for greater accuracy.

On the inner corners of any of the hexagon, equilateral-triangle or diamond blocks, sew only to the inner point (for machine piecing, this is marked by the dot transferred from the template) rather than to the edge of fabric sections *(Fig. 19).*

Steam-press points only *after* all piecing is done! Narrow points are easily distorted by a steam iron.

Mitered Corners

Many of the quilts in this book have borders with mitered corners. By following the instructions given here, you will find it easy to make neat, sharp corners. Cut the border strips according to individual instructions for each project. Place the border right side up on the table, lay the quilt, wrong side up, on top of it. Right sides will be together. The ends of the border should extend past the edge of the quilt equally on each end. Stitch the two units together, with the seam beginning and ending ¼″ in from the corners of the quilt *(Fig. 20)*. Backstitch at the start and finish of the seam. Fold the border out and press. Join borders to the other three sides in the same way. The ends of the borders should overlap *(Fig. 21)*.

Turn the top strip at one corner under so that the edges of the strips meet and a 45° angle is formed from the inner corner of the border (a) to the outer corner (b), *(Fig. 22)*. Press along the fold. Carefully bring the edges of the quilt together and stitch the border sections together, using the crease line as a guide. Sew from the inner corner to the outer edge *(Fig. 23)*. Trim off the excess fabric on the border strips and press the seam to one side.

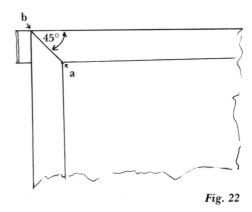

Fig. 22

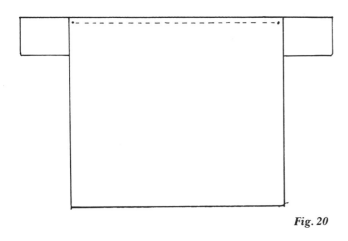

Fig. 20

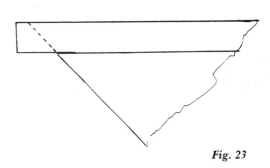

Fig. 23

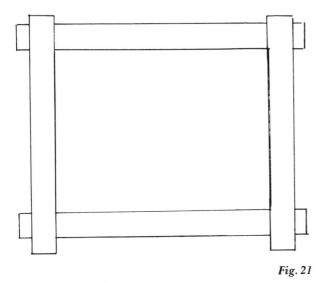

Fig. 21

For Peach Pie, Night Window and any quilt that is not square or rectangular, exactly the same process is used, but the degree of the angle formed will differ *(Fig. 24)*.

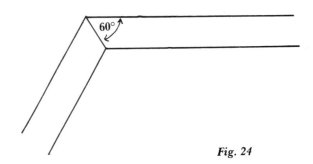

Fig. 24

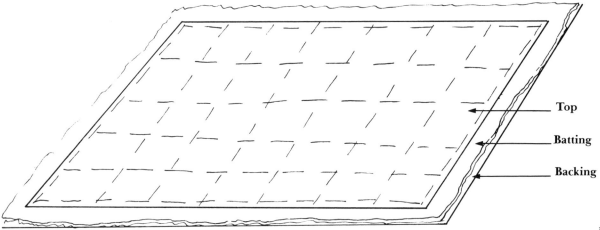

Top

Batting

Backing

Fig. 25

ASSEMBLING THE LAYERS FOR QUILTING

Cut the batting and backing fabric 2″ larger than the quilt top on all sides. Spread the layers out on a large table or cutting board—the backing, right side down, on the bottom; the batting in the middle; and the quilt top, right side up, on top. The edges of the batting and backing will extend beyond the edges of the quilt top. Pin here and there with long straight pins. Baste thoroughly with parallel stitching lines 4″ apart across both the length and width of the quilt *(Fig. 25)*. The outermost line of basting should be within ¼″ of the edge of the quilt. This will hold layers together while quilting borders.

QUILTING

Outline quilting works well with all of these designs. In wide borders, simple patterns that echo the patchwork will complement the overall design well. Uneven, ripply edges on wall quilts are often the result of quilting that is heavy in the center areas, but minimal on the border. Try to quilt evenly across all of the quilt's surface *(Fig. 26)*. When the quilting is complete, remove the basting thread and trim the batting and backing even with the edges of the quilt top.

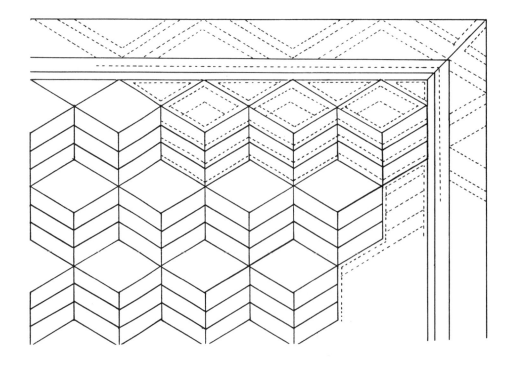

Fig. 26

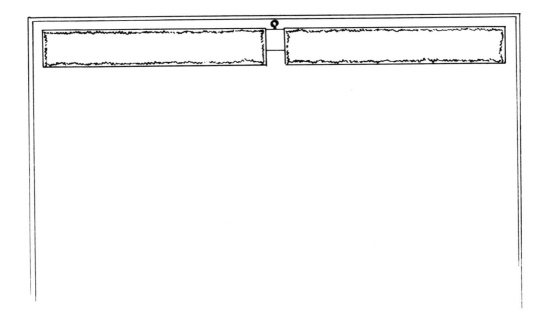

Fig. 27

BINDING

The most attractive binding is one that is the same width on the front and back.

Cut 1⅛"-wide straight or bias strips from fabric; join them to make a binding strip long enough to go around the quilt, plus a few inches extra for the corners. Turn under ¼" on one end of the binding. Pin the right side of the binding to the front of the quilt, with the raw edges matching. Using a ¼" seam, stitch around, mitering the corners and overlapping the ends. Wrap the binding to the back of the quilt; turn under the raw edge ¼" and stitch in place by hand.

SIGNING AND DATING

There are many methods of signing and dating your quilt. One easy way is to embroider your name and the year with embroidery floss on the front of the quilt in the lower right-hand corner. Backstitch or a running stitch will show up well. Or you can type your full name, the full date, the quilt's title, your address, etc. on a square of muslin and hand-stitch it to the back of the quilt. (Be certain that the typewriter ribbon ink is permanent!)

HANGING YOUR WALL QUILT

The following method works well for most projects.

Cut a strip of fabric 4" wide and as long as the top measurement of the quilt, minus 3 inches. Cut the strip of fabric in half width-wise. Fold under ½" on all edges of each section and zigzag-stitch. Pin the two sections to the back of the quilt, along the long edges, 1" down from the top edge, with about 2" between sections at the center. Hand-stitch the casing in place.

Cut a narrow board (⅜" × 2") 2" shorter than the width of the quilt. Paint the board to seal in resins that may damage the fabric over a long period of time. Sand lightly to remove rough spots. Screw a metal eyelet into the narrow edge of the board at the center *(Fig. 27)*.

Insert the board into the casing.

For some projects, especially large ones, it may be a good idea to sew a narrower casing at the bottom edge of the quilt and insert a dowel into it to keep the edge straight and flat.

Hexagon quilts will need this narrow casing across the center of the back.

SAMPLE GRIDS

Use these grids to experiment with shading to create your own three-dimensional effects. If desired, you can photocopy the grids, so that you will have several of each.

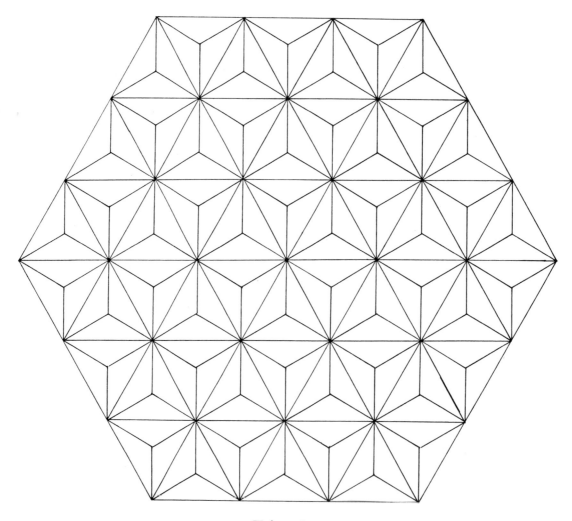

Triangle

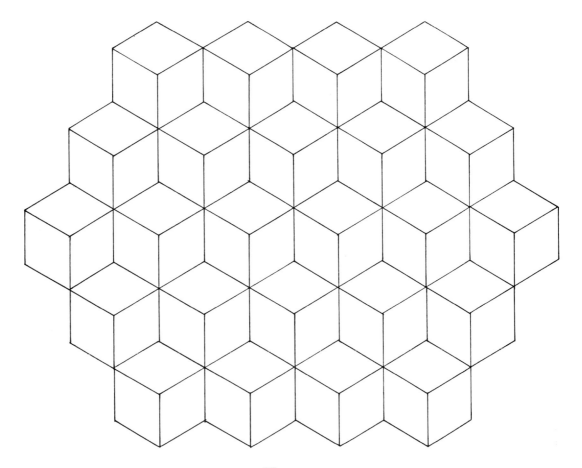

Hexagon

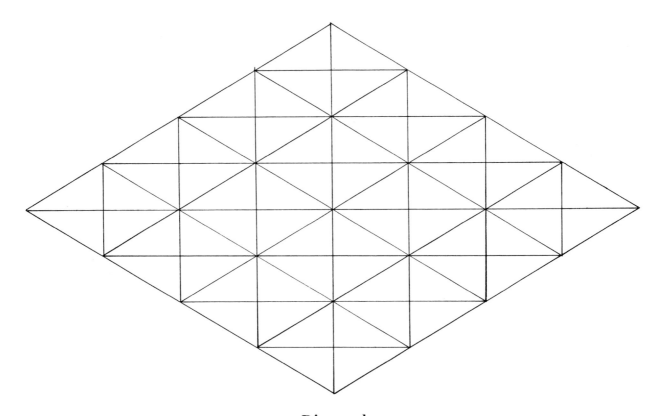

Diamond

13

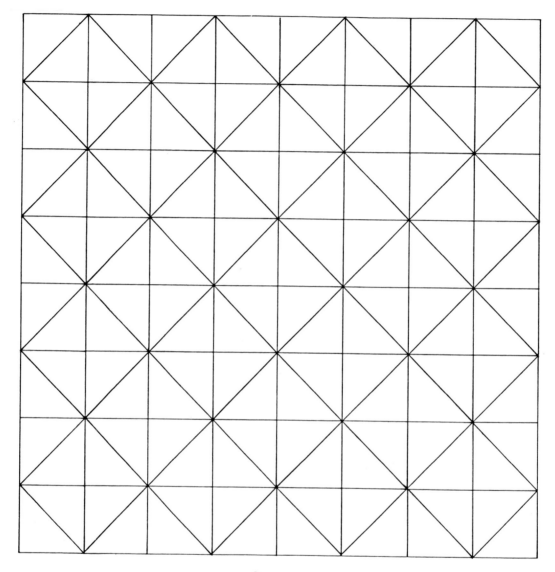

Square

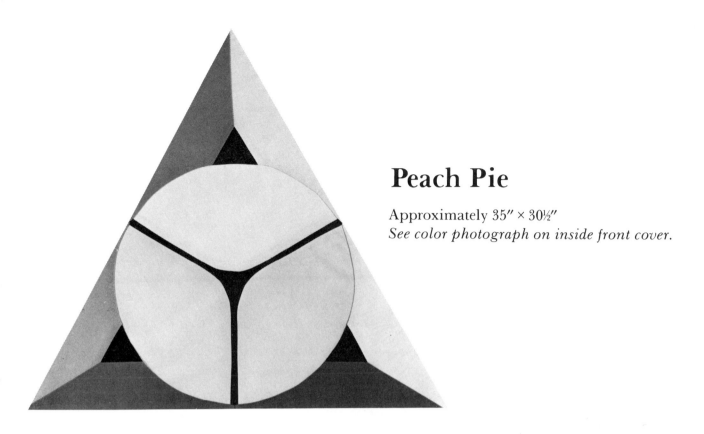

Peach Pie

Approximately 35″ × 30½″
See color photograph on inside front cover.

Because of the narrow Y-shaped pieces and the slender points at the junction of the circles, hand-piecing is recommended for this project.

Fabrics

Four shades of any color ranging from light (1) to dark (4) for the triangle points and the borders. Light (5) and medium (6) shades of a second color for the circles, plus a dark contrasting color (7) for the Y-shaped pieces—
Fabrics 1, 2, 5 and 7: ¼ yd.
Fabric 3: ¾ yd.
Fabric 4: ⅛ yd.
Fabric 6: ⅜ yd.
1 yd. fabric for backing.

Cutting

Note: The templates for pieces A and B include ¼″ seam allowance. Because it is easier to match the curves

accurately if you mark the sewing line, piece D and the inner curve of piece C do not have the seam allowance added. Be sure to allow for ¼″ seam allowance when cutting these pieces. Transfer the notches indicated on the templates to the wrong side of the fabric pieces.

Fabrics 1 and 2: Cut six A and six A reversed from each fabric. Cut four 1½″ × 19″ strips from each fabric for the borders.
Fabric 3: Cut six A and six A reversed. Cut four 1½″ × 19″ strips for the borders. Cut 1⅛″-wide strips; join to make binding 3½ yds. long.
Fabric 4: Cut 18 B.
Fabric 5: Cut six C.
Fabric 6: Cut 12 C.
Fabric 7: Cut six D.

Sew the A and A reversed pieces to the B pieces, making six of each color combination shown in *Fig. 1.* Carefully matching the notches, sew two medium and one light C piece to each D piece *(Fig. 2)* to make six circles.

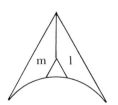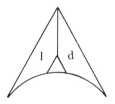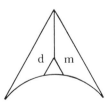

Fig. 1

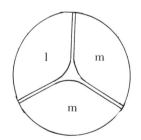

Fig. 2

Templates for this quilt are on Plates 1 and 2.

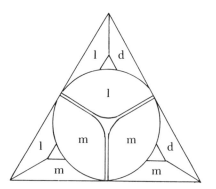
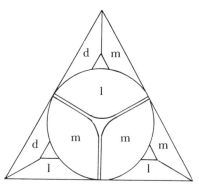
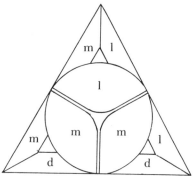

Fig. 3

Complete the large triangles by sewing the A–B points to the circles, matching the notches. Make two triangles of each color arrangement shown in *Fig. 3*.

Keeping the light sections of the circles on the inside, arrange the six triangles to form a hexagon as in *Fig. 4*. Carefully matching the seamlines of the D pieces, sew the triangles together, first sewing three triangles together to form half a hexagon, then sewing the halves together.

Sew the border strips together along the long edges in pairs, mixing the colors—light to dark, dark to medium, medium to light. You will have two of each color combination. Following *Fig. 5* for color placement, sew the borders to the quilt top, mitering the corners at a 60° angle.

Complete the quilt following the General Instructions. Sew a narrow casing across the center of the back and insert a dowel to keep the quilt flat and straight.

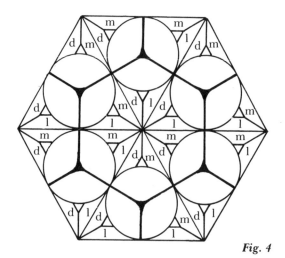

Fig. 4

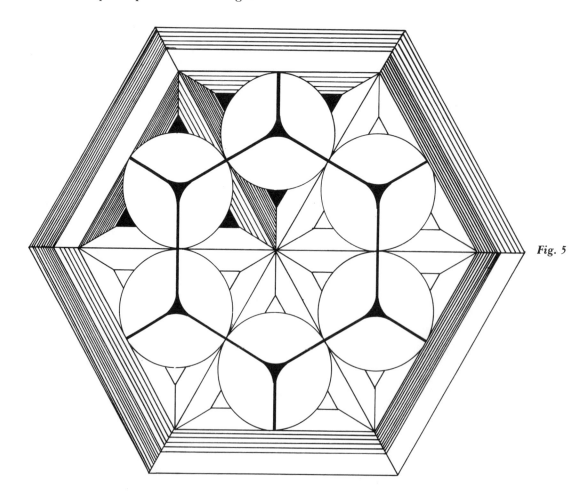

Fig. 5

Scrapboxes

Approximately 56″ × 80″
*See color photograph on
inside front cover.*

Fabrics

Scraps of solid and print fabrics in four shades ranging
  from light (1) to dark (4)—approximately 2 yds. of
  each shade for blocks.
½ yd. dark solid for edge triangles.
¼ yd. medium solid for inner border.
¾ yd. dark solid for outer border and binding.
3½ yds. fabric for backing.

Cutting

Fabrics 1–4: Following *Fig. 1* and using template A as a
  guide, quick-cut and piece 78 of square I, 39 of square
  II, 147 of square III and 74 of square IV. In addition,
  cut 18 A triangles from each fabric.
Fabric 5: Cut 32 B and four C triangles.
Inner border: Cut seven 1″-wide strips across the full
  width of the fabric. Sew two strips together to make
  an 88″–89″-long strip; repeat to make a second long
  strip. Cut one of the remaining three strips in half
  and sew one half to each of the two remaining strips.
  The borders will be trimmed to the proper length
  after they are joined to the quilt top.
Outer border and binding: Cut seven 4″-wide strips
  across the full width of the fabric. Sew two strips
  together to make an 88″–89″-long strip; repeat to
  make a second long strip. Cut one of the remaining
  three strips in half and sew one half to each of the two
  remaining strips. The borders will be trimmed to the
  proper length after they are joined to the quilt top.
  Cut 1⅛″-wide strips; join to make binding 9 yds. long.

This quilt is made up of twenty-four 12″-square blocks.
The colors in each block are the same; however, when
the blocks touch the outer edge of the quilt, dark solid
triangles are added. This will cause minor adjustments
in the color arrangement of the blocks.

Following *Fig. 2,* arrange the pieced squares to make
eight basic blocks. Join the squares in rows, then sew
the rows together.

Fig. 1

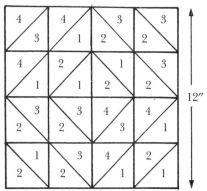

Fig. 2

Templates for this quilt are on Plate 3.

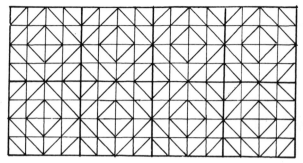

Fig. 3

Fig. 5

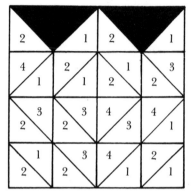

Fig. 4

Fig. 6

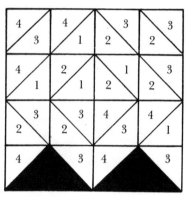

Fig. 7

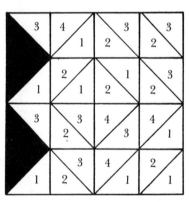

Fig. 8

Keeping all of the blocks turned in the same direction, sew them together in two rows of four blocks each; sew the rows together *(Fig. 3)*.

Make four blocks for the top edge as in *Fig. 4*. To do this, first make two rectangles by sewing an A triangle to each short edge of two B triangles *(Fig. 5)*. Sew these rectangles together along the short edge *(Fig. 6)*, then complete as for the basic block. Sew these four blocks together; sew the resulting strip to the top edge of the quilt.

In the same way, make four blocks for the lower edge following *Fig. 7*. Sew the blocks together, then sew them to the lower edge of the quilt.

Make two blocks for the left-hand edge as in *Fig. 8*; sew them together vertically. Make two blocks for the right-hand edge as in *Fig. 9*; sew them together.

Make a block for each corner following *Fig. 10*. It will be simpler to construct the corner blocks in quarters. First sew single A triangles to adjacent sides of a pieced square to make a larger triangle *(Fig. 11)*. Sew this to the C triangle to make a square *(Fig. 12)*. Make two quarters by joining pieced rectangles and pieced squares *(Fig. 13)*. For the fourth quarter, join four pieced squares together *(Fig. 14)*. Sew the quarters together to complete the block.

Sew the corner blocks to the ends of the side strips, then sew the strips to the sides of the quilt.

Sew the border strips together along the long edges; sew them to the quilt top, mitering the corners *(Fig. 15)*.

Complete the quilt following the General Instructions.

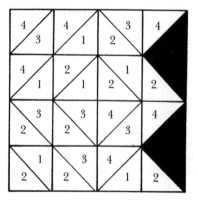

Fig. 9

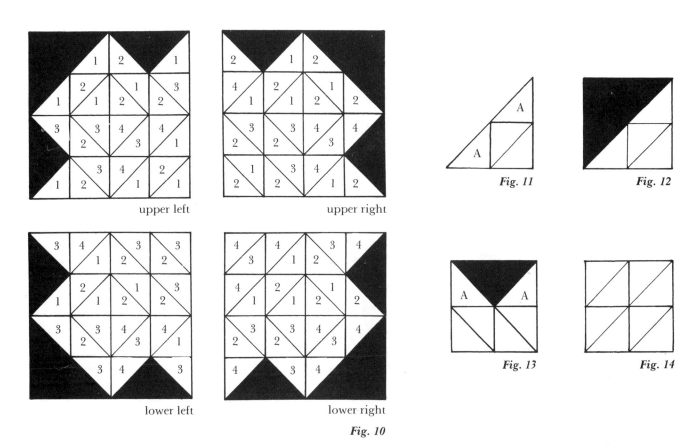

upper left   upper right

lower left   lower right

Fig. 10

Fig. 11   *Fig. 12*

Fig. 13   *Fig. 14*

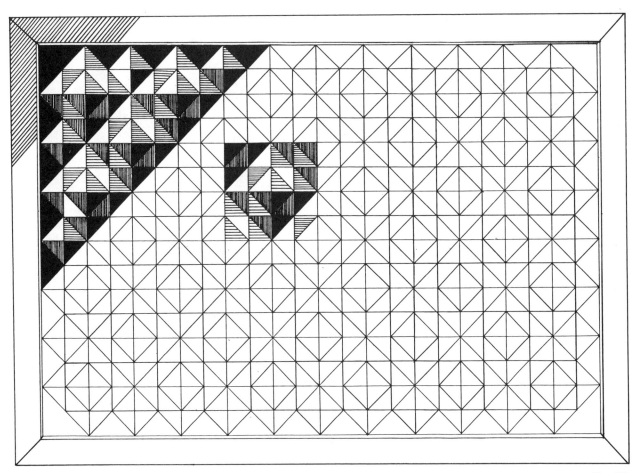

Fig. 15

Blue Star

Approximately 67″ × 39″
See color photograph on inside front cover.

Fabrics

Four different fabrics, ranging from light (1) to dark
(4)—
Fabrics 1, 2 and 3: ¾ yd. each.
Fabric 4: 1 yd. including fabric for binding.
2 yds. fabric for backing.

Cutting

Fabrics 1, 2 and 3: Cut 100 A from each fabric.
Fabric 4: Cut 1⅛″-wide bias strips; join to make binding
4½ yds. long. Cut 42 A and 14 B.

Join A triangles together as in *Fig. 1* to form 72 larger
triangles. Turning triangles as shown in *Fig. 2,* join 12
triangles to form a row. Make a total of six rows; then,

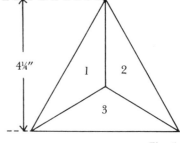

Fig. 1

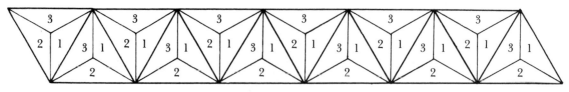

Fig. 2

Templates for this quilt are on Plate 4.

keeping the rows all turned in the same direction, sew them together as in *Fig. 3*. Turn the piece "on point" to form a diamond.

Join the remaining A triangles together, making 14 triangles of each color combination shown in *Fig. 4*. Following *Fig. 5*, sew nine pieced triangles and three B triangles together to form a row for the lower left-hand edge of the quilt. Make a row for the upper right-hand edge following *Fig. 6*. Join triangles to form rows for the upper left and lower right edges as in *Fig. 7*. Keeping the base of the dark B triangles to the outside, sew the shorter rows, then the longer rows to the quilt *(Fig. 8)*. The diamond is now complete.

Complete the quilt following the General Instructions. To hang the quilt, build a 35" × 63" diamond-shaped frame from narrow wooden boards. Glue one side of Velcro tape to the frame; sew the other side of the Velcro to the back of the quilt by hand.

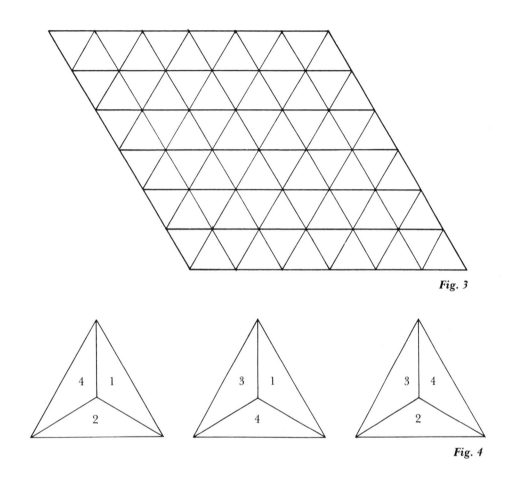

Fig. 3

Fig. 4

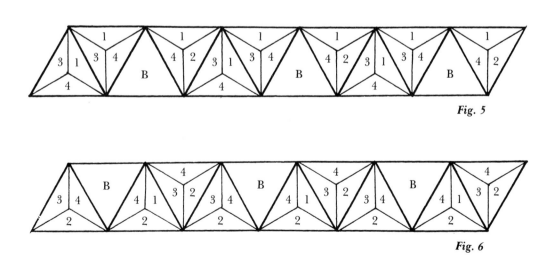

Fig. 5

Fig. 6

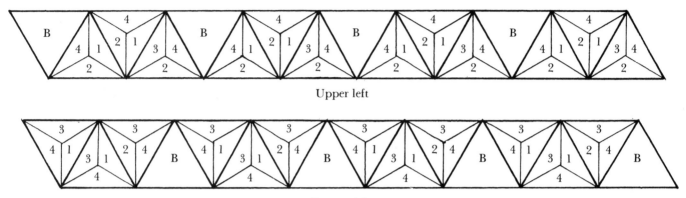

Upper left

Lower right

Fig. 7

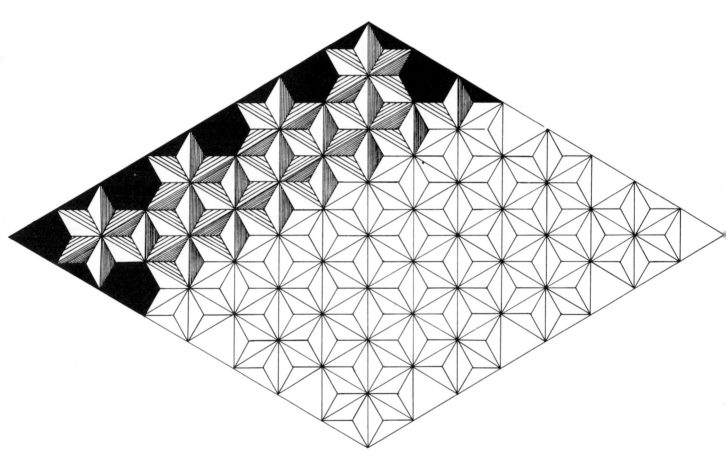

Fig. 8

Parquet Stars

Approximately 54″ × 57″
*See color photograph on inside
front cover.*

The placement of the stripes in this design adds to the optical illusion.

Many of the pieces must be "set in" in this design, and the stripes in the background pieces must be matched exactly.

Fabrics

2 yds. dark solid for outer border and diamond centers.
2 yds. evenly spaced stripe for diamonds, background and binding.
2 yds. of scraps of assorted light prints for diamonds.
2 yds. of scraps of assorted dark prints for diamonds.
¼ yd. light fabric for inner border.
4 yds. fabric for backing.

Cutting

Dark solid: Cutting along the lengthwise grain of the fabric, cut four 6″ × 72″ strips for the outer border. These strips will be trimmed to the proper length when they are joined to the quilt. Cut 84 A.
Stripe: Cut 42 B, 42 B reversed, 18 E and 18 E reversed. When cutting these pieces, place the template with the arrow parallel to the stripes, and in exactly the same position on each piece—i.e., in the exact center of a stripe, or along one edge. Cut 1⅛″-wide bias strips; join to make binding 7½ yds. long.
Light prints: Cut 99 B, 99 B reversed, 2 D and two D reversed.
Dark prints: Cut 99 B, 99 B reversed, 2 D and two D reversed.
Inner Border: Cut five 1″-wide strips across the full width of the fabric. Cut two 12″ lengths from one of

the strips. Sew one 12″ length to the end of two of the remaining border strips. These strips will be trimmed to the proper length when they are joined to the quilt.

Hexagon Block (make seven)

For each block, sew light and dark B pieces together to form a diamond, setting in the A piece by hand *(Fig. 1)*. Make four of diamond *a* and two of diamond *b*. Arrange the diamonds to form a star as in *Fig. 2*. (Sew the

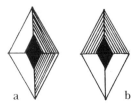

Fig. 1

Fig. 2

Templates for this quilt are on Plates 5 and 6.

23

c　　　　d　　　　e　　　　f

Fig. 3

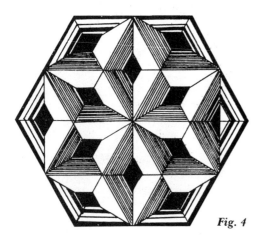

Fig. 4

diamonds together in threes to form half stars, then sew the halves together to complete the star.) For the outer diamonds, sew the striped, light and dark B pieces to the A pieces, following *Fig. 3,* and making two of diamond *c,* two of diamond *d* and one each of *e* and *f.* Keeping the stripes on the outside, sew these diamonds between the points of the star, matching light to dark *(Fig. 4).* The block is now complete. Keeping all of the blocks turned in the same direction, sew the blocks together as in *Fig. 5.*

The corners and edges of the quilt are made from the striped E triangles. Following *Fig. 6,* sew E and E reversed triangles together to form four large diamonds. Sew these diamonds to the quilt as in *Fig. 7.* Sew an E and an E reversed triangle together along the short edge as in *Fig. 8* to form a larger triangle. Repeat to form a second large triangle. Sew one to the top and one to the

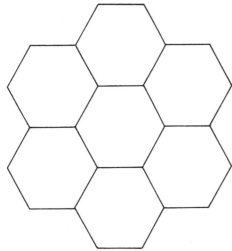

Fig. 5

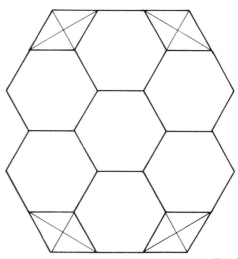

Fig. 7

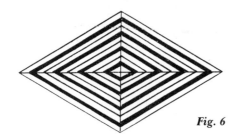

Fig. 6

Fig. 8

Fig. 9

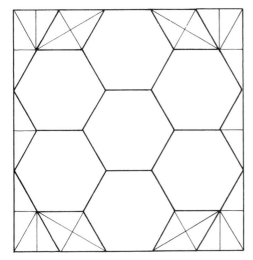

Fig. 10

bottom of the quilt. Make two of each triangle shown in *Fig. 9;* sew them to the corners of the quilt top *(Fig. 10).*

Sew the inner borders to the quilt, mitering the corners.

Measure one side of the quilt, measuring ½" outside the inner border seam. Working on the right side of one outer border strip, mark this measurement ¼" in from one long edge. With pins, mark a 45° angle out to the other edge of the border strip. Repeat this process for each outer border strip, measuring each side of the quilt separately.

Sew B pieces together as in *Fig. 11,* starting and stopping exactly on the seamlines. Make five of each color combination. Sew the five units of each color combination together to form a strip *(Fig. 12).* Join the remaining B pieces to the D pieces to form eight different corner units as in *Fig. 13.* Join the corners to the patched strips, joining *a* to *a, b* to *b, c* to *c* and *d* to *d.*

Pin one patched strip to each outer border, matching the long straight edge of the patched strip to the marked inner edge of the outer border *(Fig. 14).* The ends of the patched strips should extend ¼" beyond the 45° lines marked on the outer border. You may find it necessary to adjust the seamlines on the individual units of the patched strip to make it fit properly. Baste along the straight edge and the 45° line. Turn under the remaining edges of the patched strip and appliqué it to the outer border. Sew the borders to the quilt, mitering the corners *(Fig. 15).*

Complete the quilt following the General Instructions.

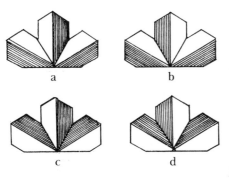

Fig. 11

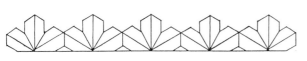

Fig. 12

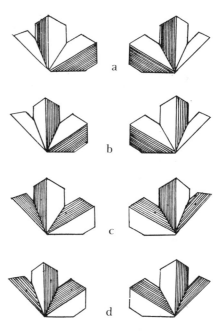

Fig. 13

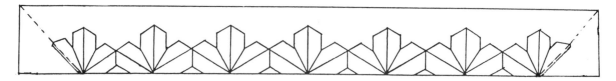

Fig. 14

Fig. 15

Night Window

Approximately 65″ × 57″
See color photograph on front cover.

Fabrics

4 yds. assorted light prints (1).
1½ yds. assorted medium prints (2).
2½ yds. assorted dark prints (3).
⅝ yd. dark solid (4).
⅜ yd. medium stripe for inner border.
⅜ yd. light print for outer border.
¼ yd. medium print for outer border.
¼ yd. dark print for outer border.
4 yds. fabric for backing.

Cutting

Fabric 1: Cut 225 B.
Fabric 2: Cut 75 B.
Fabric 3: Cut 150 B.
Fabric 4: Cut 150 A.
Inner border: Cut six 2″ × 35″ strips from striped fabric.
Outer border and binding: Cut six 3¼″ × 35″ strips—
    three light, one medium and two dark. For the quilt
    shown, the outer border is pieced by cutting 1⅛″-wide
    strips of various fabrics of each shade and sewing
    them together along the long edges. From the
    medium print, cut strips 1⅛″ wide; join to make
    binding six yds. long.

Sew the A and B pieces together to form triangles as in
Fig. 1, making 75 of each color combination shown in
Fig. 2.

The quilt top is constructed in horizontal rows,
alternating upward-pointing and downward-pointing
triangles. The *a* triangles will always point up and the *b*
triangles will always point down.

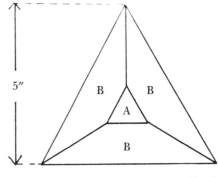

5″

B   B
A
B

Fig. 1

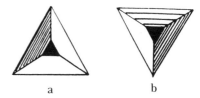

a   b

Fig. 2

Templates for this quilt are on Plate 7.

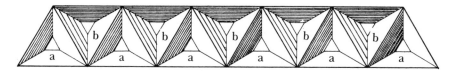

Fig. 3

Row 1 (Fig. 3): 11 triangles, six *a* and five *b*.
Row 2: 13 triangles, seven *a* and six *b*.
Row 3: 15 triangles, eight *a* and seven *b*.
Row 4: 17 triangles, nine *a* and eight *b*.
Row 5: 19 triangles, ten *a* and nine *b*.
Row 6: 19 triangles, ten *b* and nine *a*.
Row 7: 17 triangles, nine *b* and eight *a*.
Row 8: 15 triangles, eight *b* and seven *a*.
Row 9: 13 triangles, seven *b* and six *a*.
Row 10: 11 triangles, six *b* and five *a*.

Arrange the ten rows following *Fig. 4;* sew them together.

Sew the inner and outer border strips together along the long edges. Sew them to the quilt top, mitering the corners at a 60° angle *(Fig. 5)*. The top and left-hand side of the quilt should have a light outer border; the top right side should have a medium outer border and the remaining two sides should have a dark outer border.

Complete the quilt following the General Instructions. Sew a narrow casing across the center of the back and insert a dowel to keep the quilt flat and straight.

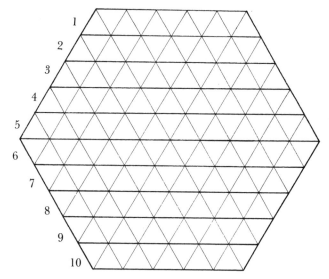

Fig. 4

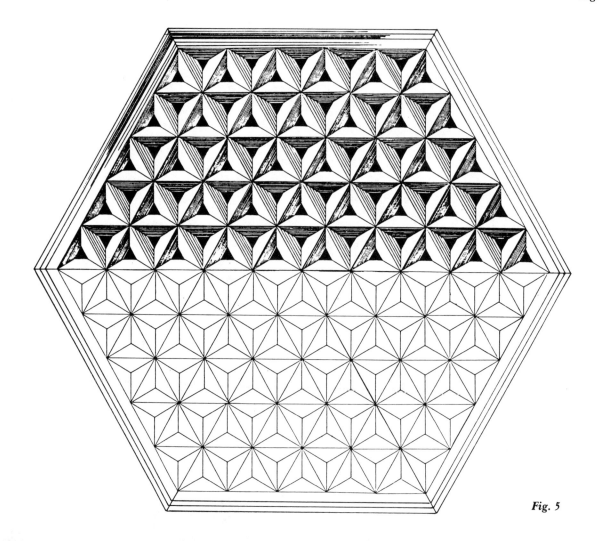

28

Fig. 5

Tumbling Blocks, Variation I

Approximately 31″ × 21″
See color photograph on inside back cover.

Fabrics

¼ yd. each of four different fabrics ranging from light (1) to dark (4) (we used scraps of many different fabrics for 1, 2 and 3).
¼ yd. light fabric for inner border.
¼ yd. medium fabric for center border.
¼ yd. dark fabric for outer border and binding.
¾ yd. fabric for backing.

Cutting

Fabrics 1, 2 and 3: Cut 26 A and 13 B from each fabric.
Fabric 4: Cut ten C and four D.
Inner border: Cut two strips ¾″ × 34″ and two strips ¾″ × 24″.
Center border: Cut two strips 1″ × 34″ and two strips 1″ × 24″.
Outer border and binding: Cut two strips 3″ × 34″ and two strips 3″ × 24″. Cut 1⅛″-wide bias strips; join to make binding 3½ yds. long.

Hexagon Block (make 13)

For each block, join A and B pieces to make three diamonds as in *Fig. 1.* Join these diamonds as in *Fig. 2* to complete the blocks.

Templates for this quilt are on Plate 8.

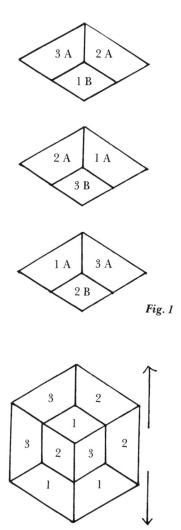

Fig. 1

Fig. 2

Making sure that all of the blocks are turned as in *Fig. 2*, sew the hexagons together along the side edges *(Fig. 3)* to form two rows of four and one row of five. Be sure to start and stop exactly on the seamlines so that the rows can be joined easily.

Sew the rows together, adding the C and D pieces along the edges *(Fig. 4)*.

Join the inner, center and outer border strips along the long edge; sew them to the quilt, mitering the corners *(Fig. 5)*.

Complete the quilt following the General Instructions.

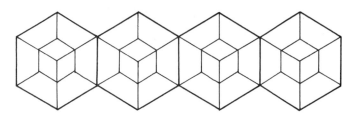

Fig. 3

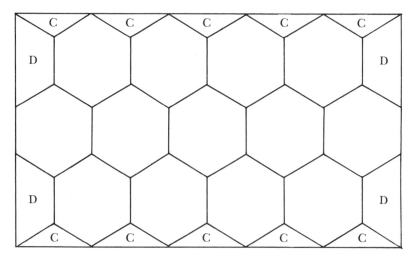

Fig. 4

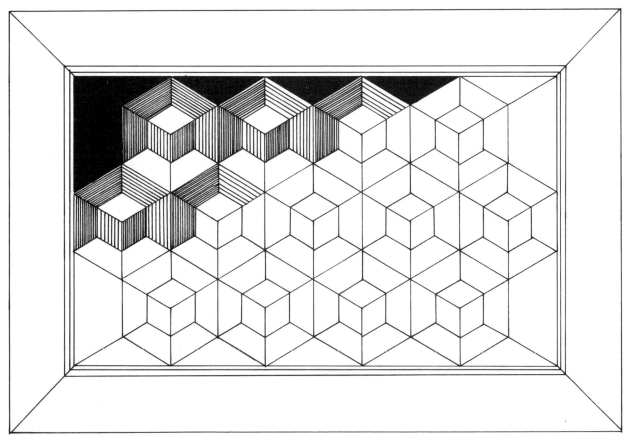

Fig. 5

Tumbling Blocks, Variation II

Approximately 48″ × 23½″
See color photograph on inside back cover.

In the quilt shown, shades of beige, gray and blue were combined in the striped areas—light on one side, medium on the other. Dark blue was used for the large diamonds. The striped sections are quick-pieced and cut.

Fabrics

Light (1) and medium (2) shades of two different colors (a and b), plus light (1), medium (2) and dark (3) shades of a third color (c)—
  Fabric 1a: ⅝ yd. for blocks, corners, edges and center border.
  Fabrics 1b, 1c and 2b: ⅛ yd. each for blocks.
  Fabric 2a: ⅝ yd. for blocks, outer border and binding.
  Fabric 2c: ⅜ yd. for blocks and inner border.
  Fabric 3c: ¼ yd. for large diamonds.
1½ yds. fabric for backing.

Cutting

Fabric 1a: Cut four 1½″-wide strips across the full width of the fabric for the center border. Cut 18″ from one end of two of the strips; sew one 18″ length to each of the other two strips. Cut two 1½″-wide strips across the full width of the fabric for the blocks. Cut a 14″ square; cut in half diagonally for lower corners. Cut ten B, one C and one C reversed.
Fabrics 1b, 2b and 1c: From each fabric, cut two 1½″-wide strips across the full width of the fabric for the blocks.
Fabric 2a: Cut four 3″-wide strips across the full width of the fabric for the outer borders. Cut 18″ from one end of two of the border strips; sew one to each of the other two border strips. Cut two 1½″-wide strips across the full width of the fabric for the blocks. Cut 1⅛″-wide strips; join them to make a binding 5 yds. long.

Fabric 2c: Cut four 1″-wide strips across the full width of the fabric for the inner borders. Cut 18″ from one end of two of the border strips; sew one 18″ length to each of the other two border strips. Cut two 1½″-wide strips across the full width of the fabric for the blocks.
Fabric 3c: Cut 18 A.

Diamond Block (make 18)

Sew a 1a, 1b and 1c strip together along the long edges *(Fig. 1)*. Repeat to form another strip. Sew the 2a, 2b and 2c strips together in the same manner *(Fig. 2)*. Following *Fig. 3,* cut 18 A diamonds from the light pieced strips and 18 A diamonds from the medium pieced

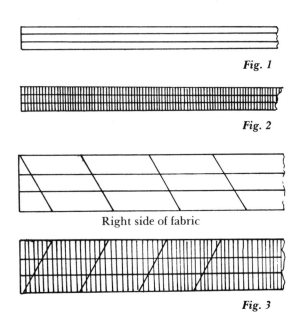

Fig. 1

Fig. 2

Right side of fabric

Fig. 3

Templates for this quilt are on Plate 9.

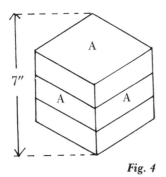

Fig. 4

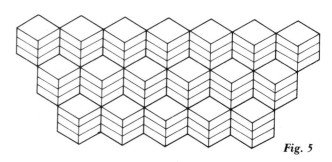

Fig. 5

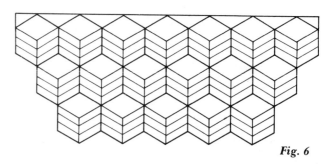

Fig. 6

Fig. 7

strips. Note that the template is turned in a different direction for the light and medium strips.

Sew the light and medium diamonds together along one short edge; sew the dark A diamond to the top to complete the block *(Fig. 4)*.

Keeping the blocks all turned in the same direction, and carefully matching the seam allowances of the strips, sew seven blocks together along the side edge to form a strip. Be careful to start and stop exactly on the seam allowance so that the rows can be joined easily. Make a strip of six blocks, then sew the remaining five blocks together. Carefully sew the three rows together *(Fig. 5)*. Sew the B triangles along the top and bottom edges; sew the C triangles to the top corners *(Fig. 6)*.

For the bottom corners, place the two large light triangles under the lower corners of the quilt, lining up the edges with the straight side and lower edges *(Fig. 7)*. Turn under the edges of the blocks and appliqué them to the triangles.

Sew the inner, center and outer border strips together, sew them to the quilt, mitering the corners *(Fig. 8)*.

Complete the quilt following the General Instructions.

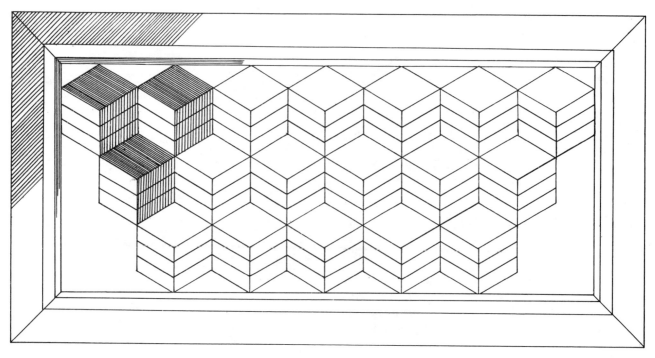

Fig. 8

Tumbling Blocks, Variation III

Approximately 38¾″ × 27½″
See color photograph on inside back cover.

Fabrics

Five fabrics ranging from light (1) to dark (5)—
  Fabrics 1, 2 and 5: ¼ yd. each for blocks.
  Fabric 3: 1 yd. for blocks, outer border and binding.
  Fabric 4: ½ yd. for blocks and inner border.
⅜ yd. light fabric (6) for corners and edges. We used the
  same fabric as for Fabric 1.
1 yd. fabric for backing.

Fig. 1

Cutting

Fabrics 1 and 2: Cut 20 D from each fabric.
Fabric 3: Cut two strips 2½″ × 42″ and two strips 2½″ × 31″
  for outer border. Cut 1⅛″-wide strips; join to make
  binding 4 yds. long. Cut 44A.
Fabric 4: Cut two strips 1½″ × 42″ and two strips 1½″ × 31″
  for outer border. Cut 44 A.
Fabric 5: Cut 40 B and 24 C.
Fabric 6: Cut two rectangles 10¼″ × 8″; cut each in half
  diagonally following *Fig. 1*. You will only need one
  of the halves from each rectangle. Cut six E, one F
  and one F reversed.

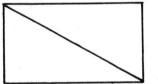

Fig. 2

Diamond Block (make 16)

For each block, first sew one 3 A and one 4 A piece to a 5
C piece to make a diamond *(Fig. 2)*. Sew a 1 D piece to a

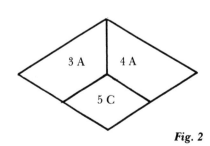
Templates for this quilt are on Plates 10 and 14.

33

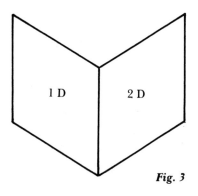

Fig. 3

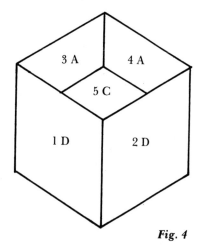

Fig. 4

2 D piece *(Fig. 3)*, then sew the pieced diamond to the top of this unit *(Fig. 4)*. Sew a 4 A piece to a 5 B piece to form a triangle *(Fig. 5)*; sew the triangle to the right-hand side of the block *(Fig. 6)*. Sew a 3 A piece to a 5 B piece *(Fig. 7)*; sew it to the left-hand side of the block *(Fig. 8)*.

Following *Fig. 9*, make two partial blocks for the left edge of the quilt and two for the right edge. Make two edge triangles following *Fig. 5* and two following *Fig. 6*. Make four small diamonds following *Fig. 2*.

Arrange the blocks, partial blocks, triangles, small diamonds and E and F triangles as in *Fig. 10*. Sew the pieces together in diagonal rows, then sew the rows together. Sew the large Fabric 6 triangles to the lower edges to make a rectangle *(Fig. 11)*. Sew the inner and outer border strips together along the long edges, then sew the borders to the quilt, mitering the corners *(Fig. 12)*.

Complete the quilt following the General Instructions.

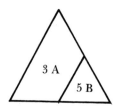

Fig. 7

Fig. 5

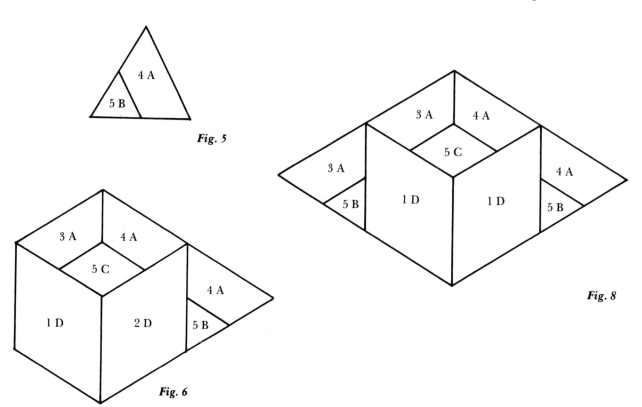

Fig. 8

Fig. 6

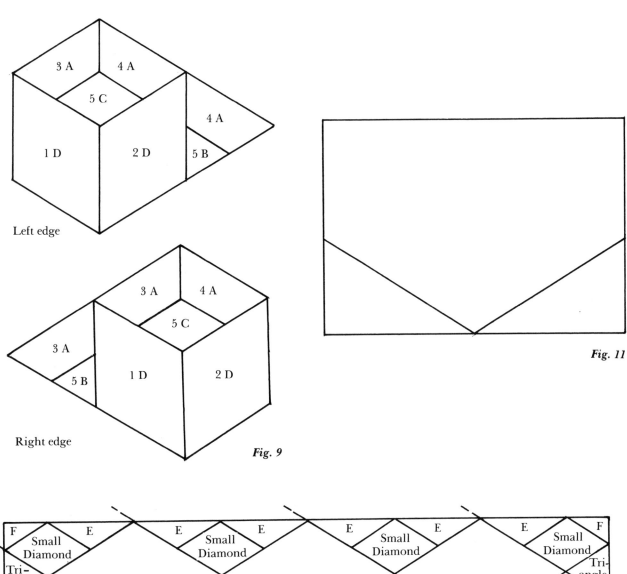

Left edge

Right edge

Fig. 9

Fig. 11

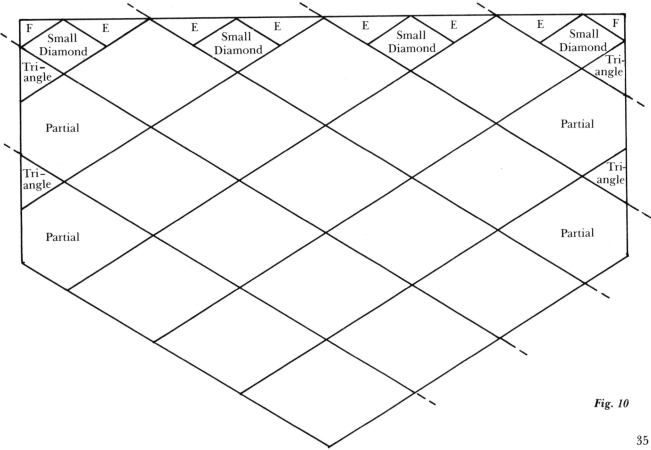

Fig. 10

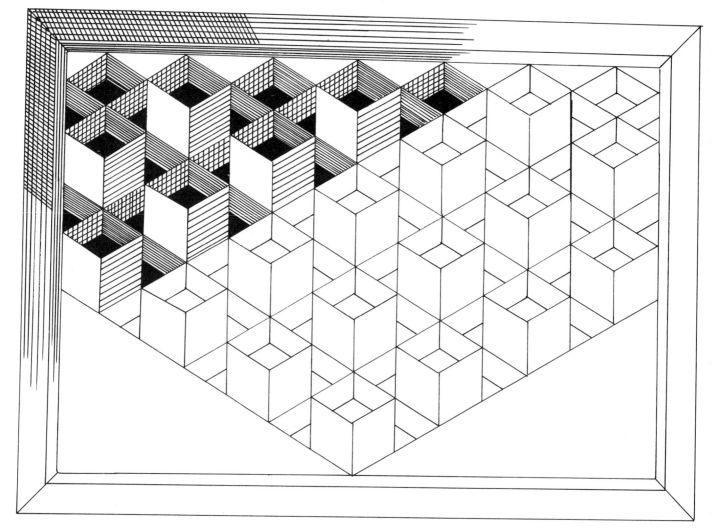

Fig. 12

Shadow Box, Variation II

Approximately 33½″ × 27½″
See color photograph on inside front cover.

Fabrics

Seven shades of one color, ranging from light (1) to dark
(7)—
   Fabrics 1, 2, 3, 4, 5 and 6: ¼ yd. each.
   Fabric 7: ¾ yd. including fabric for wide border and
   binding.
1 yd. fabric for backing.

Note: Instructions are given here for a solid border. To
make a shaded border as shown, buy additional yardage
of color desired and see instructions below.

Cutting

Fabrics 1 and 2: Following instructions for quick-
   cutting and piecing, mark 2⅞″ squares on the fabrics;
   cut 45 A triangles joined to make larger triangles
   *(Fig. 1).** From fabric 1, cut two strips 1″ × 37″ and
   two strips 1″ × 32″ for center border.
Fabrics 3 and 4: Following instructions for quick-
   cutting and piecing, mark 2⅞″ squares on the fabrics;
   cut 45 A triangles joined to make larger triangles
   *(Fig. 2).** From fabric 3, cut two strips 1¼″ × 37″ and
   two strips 1¼″ × 32″ for inner border.
Fabric 5: Cut 11 B and four C.
Fabric 6: Cut 16 B and three C.
Fabric 7: Cut four A, four B and 16 C. Cut two strips 3¼″
   × 37″ and two strips 3¼″ × 32″ for outer border. Cut
   1⅛″-wide strips; join to make binding 3¾″ yds. long.

*If you prefer to use traditional piecing methods, cut 45 A
triangles each from fabrics 1, 2, 3 and 4. Join to make larger
triangles.

Sew the pieced triangles together to form squares as in
Fig. 3. Arrange the pieced squares, plain squares and B

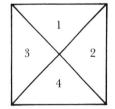

Fig. 1

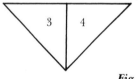

Fig. 2

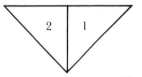

Fig. 3

Templates for this quilt are on Plate 11.

Fig. 4

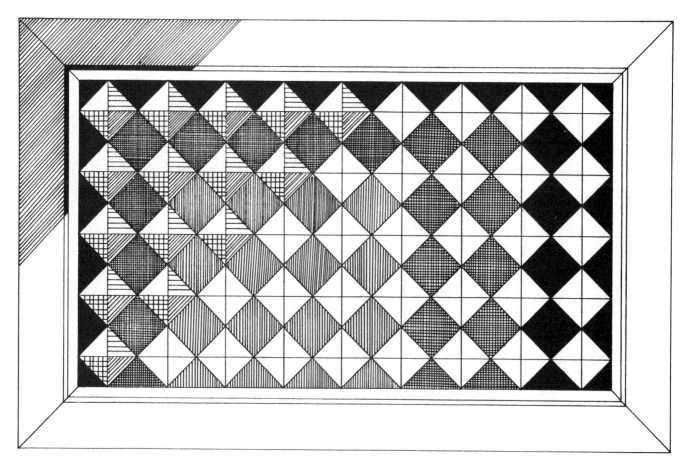

Fig. 5

and C triangles as shown in *Fig. 4*. Sew them together in diagonal rows, then sew the rows together.

Sew the inner, center and outer border strips together along the long edges to form 4½″-wide strips. Sew the borders to the quilt mitering the corners *(Fig. 5)*.

Note: To make a pieced, shaded border, cut 3¼″-wide strips from colors as desired. To join them, place the strips at right angles to one another, with right sides together. Stitch across at a 45° angle from the corner of the top strip to the corner of the bottom strip *(Fig. 6)*. Trim the seam allowance to ¼″ and press the seam to one side. Trim the border strips to the correct lengths.

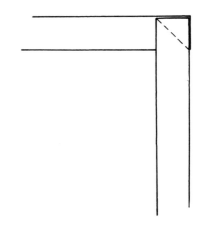

Fig. 6

Shadow Box, Variation III

Approximately 29½″ × 22″
See color photograph on inside back cover.

Templates for this quilt are on Plate 12.

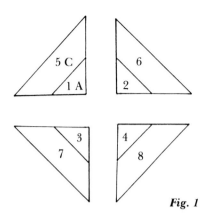

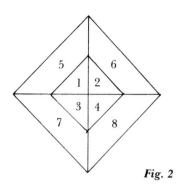

Fig. 1

Fig. 2

Fabrics

⅛ yd. each or scraps of nine different fabrics for blocks—four shades of one color ranging from light (1) to dark (4); four shades of a second color ranging from light (5) to dark (8); plus one very dark accent fabric (9).
⅛ yd. fabric for inner border.
½ yd. fabric for outer border and binding.
¾ yd. fabric for backing.

Note: The quilt illustrated was a "work in progress" and does not show the border. The finished quilt has a narrow inner border of light fabric and a wider outer border of medium fabric.

Cutting

Fabrics 1–4: Cut 12 A of each fabric.
Fabrics 5–8: Cut 12 B and six C of each fabric.
Fabric 9: Cut 12 A and six D.

Inner border: Cut two strips 1″ × 33″ and two strips 1″ × 25″.
Outer border and binding: Cut two strips 3¼″ × 33″ and two strips 3¼″ × 25″. Cut 1⅛″-wide strips; join to make binding 3 yds. long.

This quilt is made up of two different blocks set on the diagonal.

Block I (make six)

Sew the A and C pieces together to make four triangles as in *Fig. 1.* Sew the four triangles together to complete the block *(Fig. 2).*

Block II (make two)

Sew A and B pieces together as in *Fig. 3,* making one of each color combination shown. Sew these units together in pairs *(Fig. 4),* then sew a D triangle to the outer

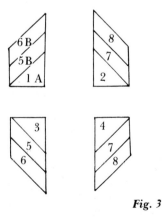

Fig. 3

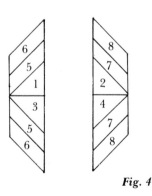

Fig. 4

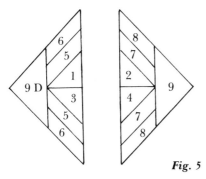

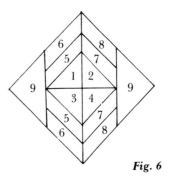

Fig. 5   **Fig. 6**

edge to form a larger triangle *(Fig. 5).* Sew the two large triangles together to form a square *(Fig. 6).*

Begin a third block, but do not join the two large triangles. These will be used at the side edges of the quilt.

Make two each of the half-blocks shown in *Fig. 7* for the upper and lower edges of the quilt. Make corner blocks as shown in *Fig. 8.* Sew the blocks and partial blocks together in diagonal rows as shown in *Fig. 9;* then sew the rows together.

Sew the inner and outer border strips together along the long edges. Sew the borders to the quilt, mitering the corners.

Complete the quilt following the General Instructions.

An attractive variation of this design can be made by using fabric 9 for all of the triangles at the outer edges of the quilt center *(Fig. 10).*

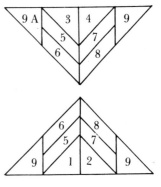

Fig. 7

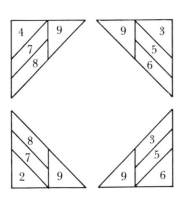

Fig. 8

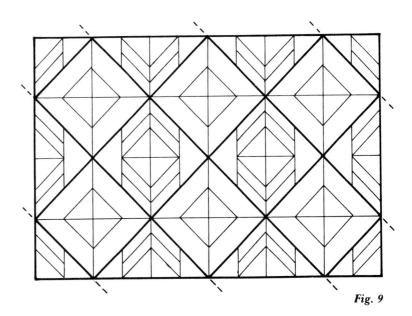

Fig. 9

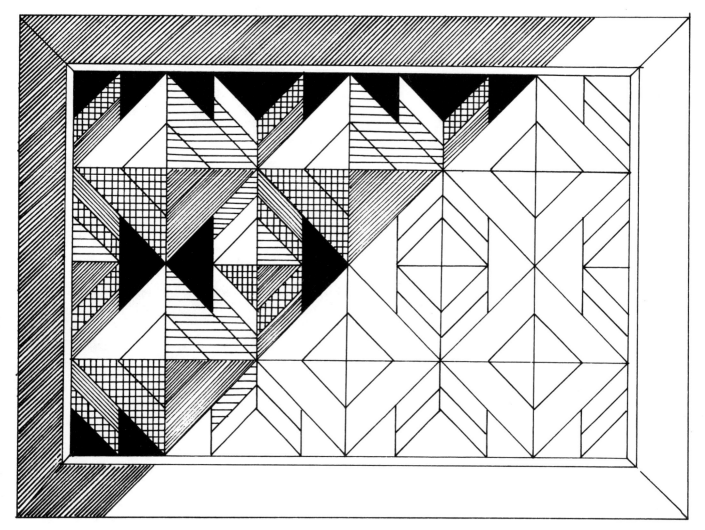

Fig. 10

Three by Three, Variation I

Approximately 36″ × 21″
See color photograph on inside back cover.

Fabrics

Five shades of one color, ranging from light (1) to dark
(5)—
Fabrics 1, 3 and 5: ¼ yd.
Fabric 2: ½ yd.
Fabric 4: ⅛ yd.
¼ yd. of a dark shade of a contrasting color (6).
¾ yd. fabric for backing.

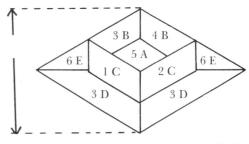

Fig. 1

Cutting

Fabric 1: Cut two rectangles 13¾″ × 8″; cut each in half
diagonally to form corner triangles *(Fig. 1)*.
Fabric 2: Cut nine C reversed and nine D.
Fabric 3: Cut nine B and nine D reversed.
Fabric 4: Cut nine B.
Fabric 5: Cut nine A. Cut four strips 2″ × 21″ and four
strips 2″ × 14″ for outer border.
Fabric 6: Cut nine E and nine E reversed. Cut four strips
1″ × 21″ and four strips 1″ × 14″ for inner border. Cut
1⅛″-wide strips; join to make binding 3½ yds. long.

Make nine diamond-shaped blocks following *Fig. 2*.
Keeping all of the block turned in the same direction,

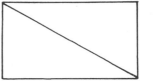

Fig. 2

Templates for this quilt are on Plate 13.

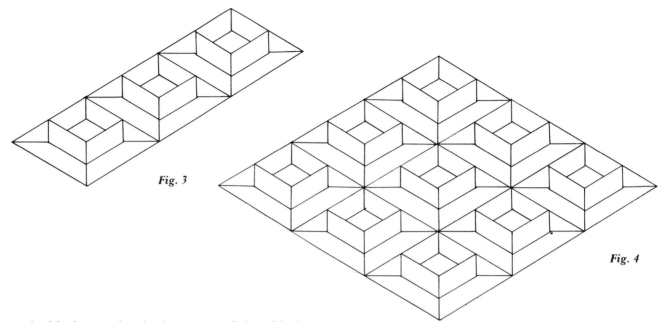

Fig. 3

Fig. 4

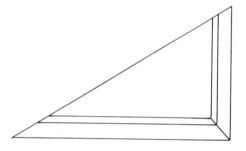

sew the blocks together in three rows of three blocks each *(Fig. 3)*. Sew the rows together to form a large diamond *(Fig. 4)*.

Sew the inner border strips to the outer border along the long edges. Sew these border strips to adjacent sides of each large corner triangle, mitering the corners *(Fig. 5)*. Trim the ends of the border strips so that the angle created by the diagonal edge of the triangle is continued. Sew these triangles to the edges of the quilt center *(Fig. 6)*.

Complete the quilt following the General Instructions.

Fig. 5

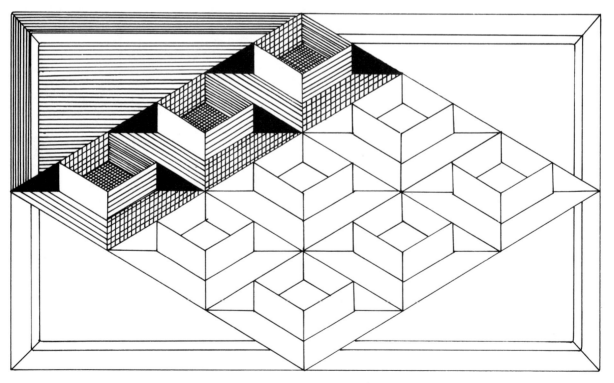

Fig. 6

Three by Three, Variation II

Approximately 32½″ × 20½″
See color photograph on inside back cover.

Fabrics

Five different fabrics for blocks, ranging from light (1)
  to dark (5)—
  Fabrics 1 and 4: ¼ yd.
  Fabric 2: ⅛ yd.
  Fabric 3: ½ yd.
  Fabric 5: ⅜ yd.
¼ yd. fabric for inner border (we used fabric 4).
⅜ yd. dark solid for outer border and binding.
¾ yd. fabric for backing.

Cutting

Fabric 1: Cut six B and nine G.
Fabric 2: Cut six B and nine F.
Fabric 3: Cut six A, six C and nine D reversed.
Fabric 4: Cut six A, six C and nine D.
Fabric 5: Cut nine E, four H, two I and two I reversed.
Inner border: Cut two strips 2″ × 35″ and two strips 1″
  × 24″.
Outer border and binding: Cut two strips 2″ × 35″ and
  two strips 2″ × 24″. Cut 1⅛″-wide strips; join to make
  binding 3½ yds. long.

This wall quilt is made up of two different diamond-
shaped blocks, plus several partial blocks.

Block I (make 4)

Sew A, B and C pieces together to form two triangles as
in *Fig. 1.* Sew the two triangles together as in *Fig. 2* to
complete the block.

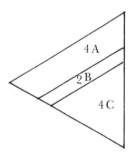 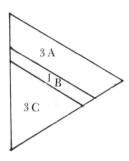

Fig. 1

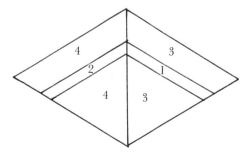

Fig. 2

Templates for this quilt are on Plates 14, 15 and 16.

45

Block II (make 9)

Sew D and E pieces together to form a triangle as in *Fig. 3*. Sew F and G pieces together to form a triangle as in *Fig. 4*. Sew the two triangles together to complete the block *(Fig. 5)*.

Partial Blocks

Sew remaining A, B and C pieces together to form triangles as before.

Arrange the blocks, partial blocks and H and I triangles as in *Fig. 6*. Sew the pieces together in diagonal rows, then sew the rows together.

Sew the inner and outer border strips together along the long edges. Sew them to the quilt, mitering the corners *(Fig. 7)*.

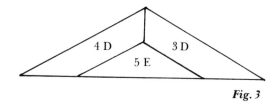

Fig. 3

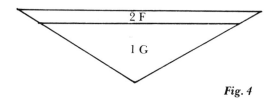

Fig. 4

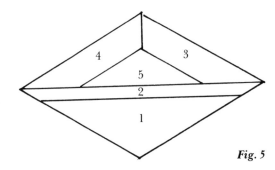

Fig. 5

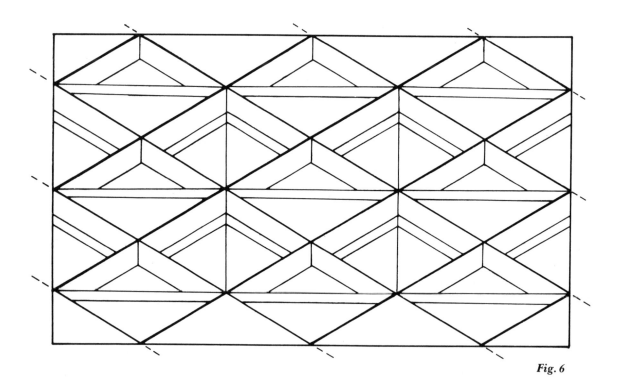

Fig. 6

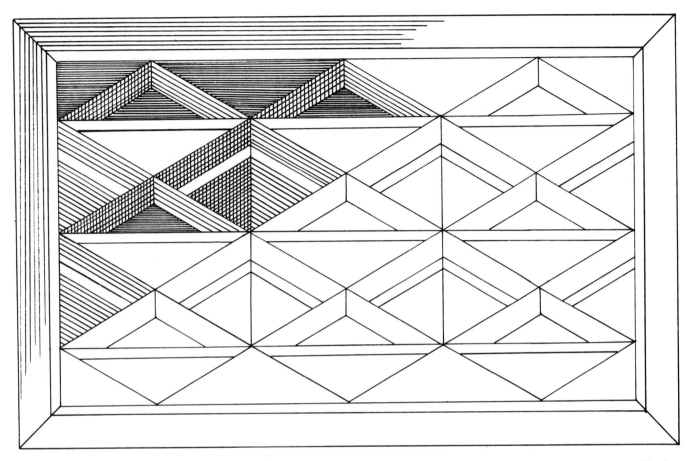

Fig. 7

Peach Pie

The seam allowance has not been added to template D or to the inner edge of template C. Be sure to allow for ¼″ seam allowance when cutting these pieces.

D

Peach Pie

C

Peach Pie

Plate 1

Peach Pie

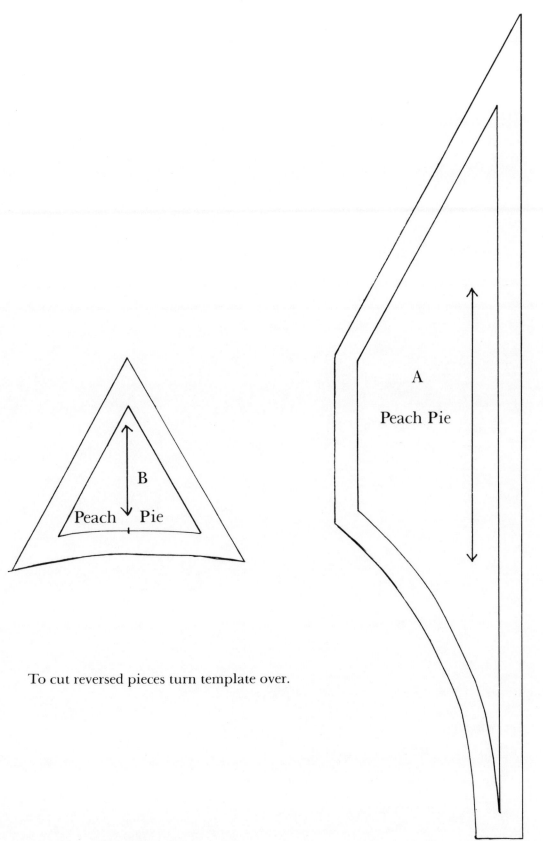

To cut reversed pieces turn template over.

Instructions for this quilt begin on page 15.

Plate 2

Scrapboxes

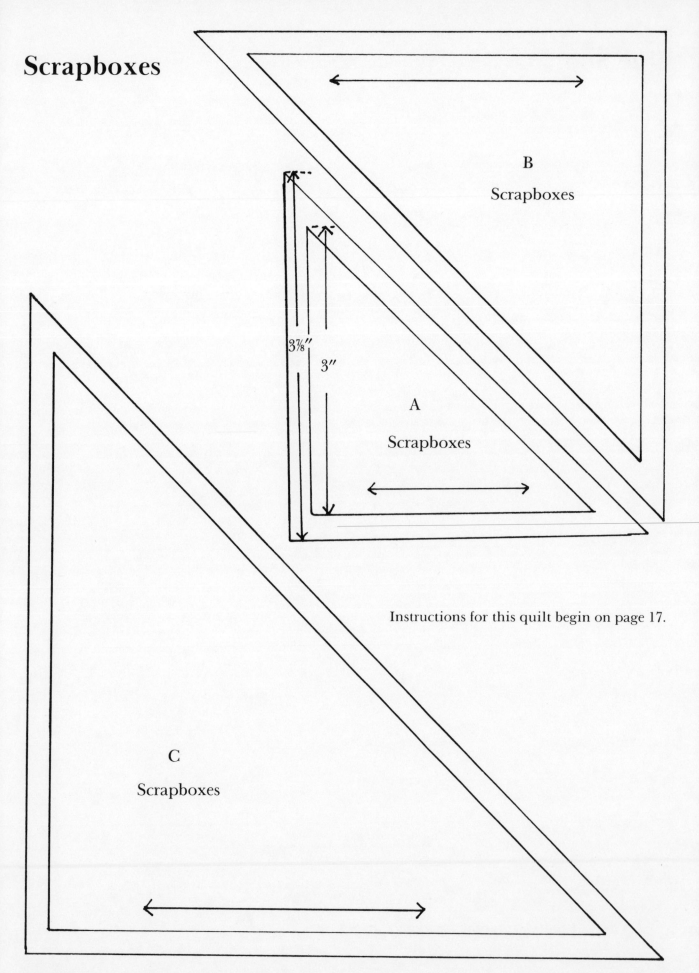

B

Scrapboxes

3⅞″   3″

A

Scrapboxes

Instructions for this quilt begin on page 17.

C

Scrapboxes

Plate 3

Blue Star

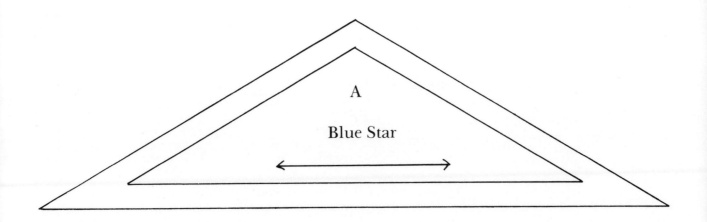

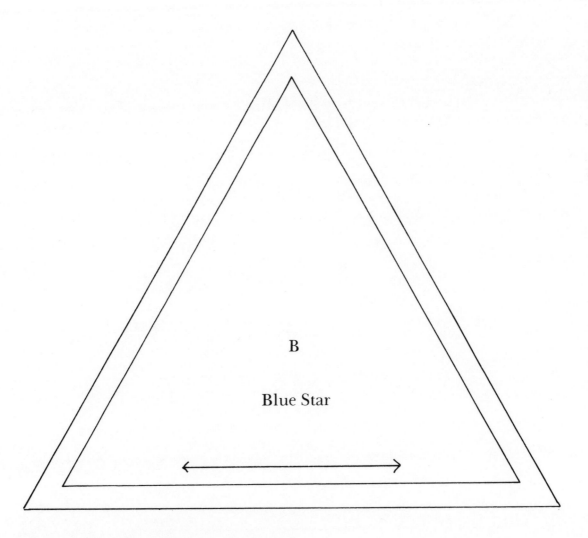

Instructions for this quilt begin on page 20.

Plate 4

Parquet Stars

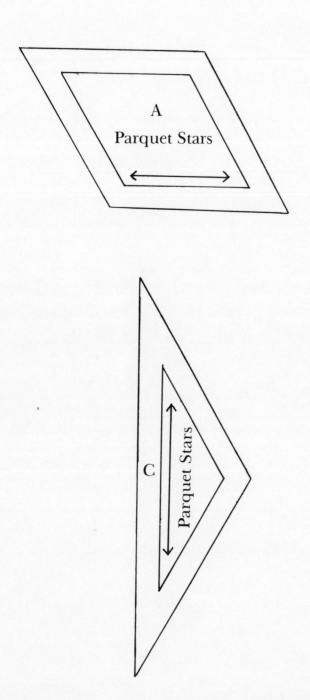

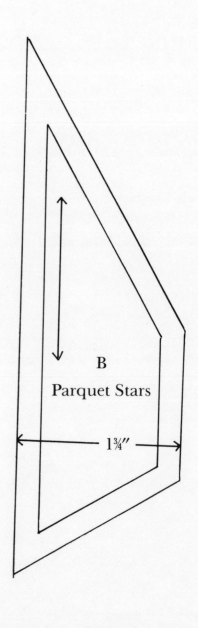

To cut reversed pieces turn template over.

Plate 5

Instructions for this quilt begin on page 23.

Parquet Stars

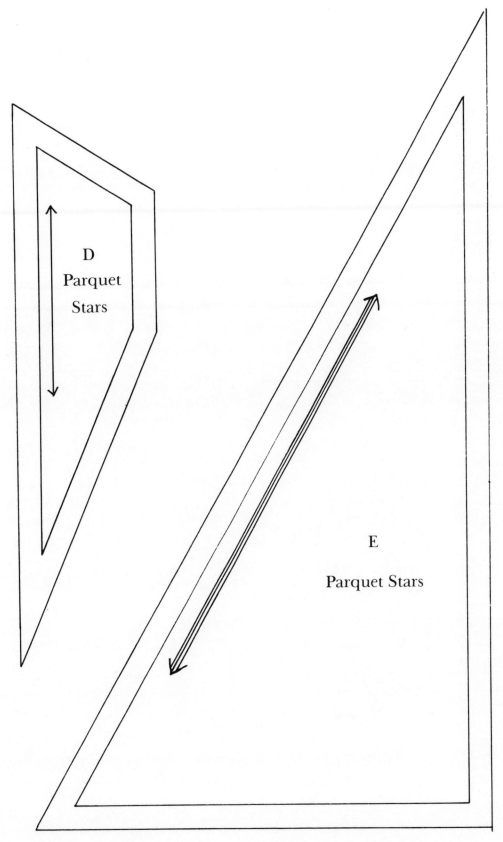

D
Parquet
Stars

E

Parquet Stars

Plate 6

Night Window

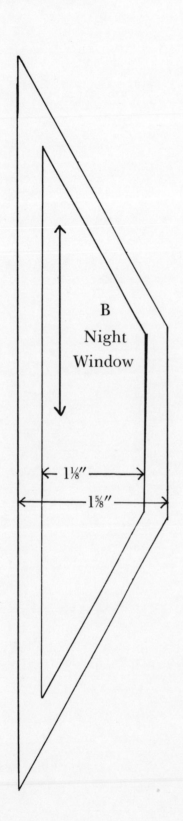

B
Night
Window

1⅛″

1⅝″

A
Night Window

Instructions for this quilt begin on page 27.

Plate 7

Tumbling Blocks, Variation I

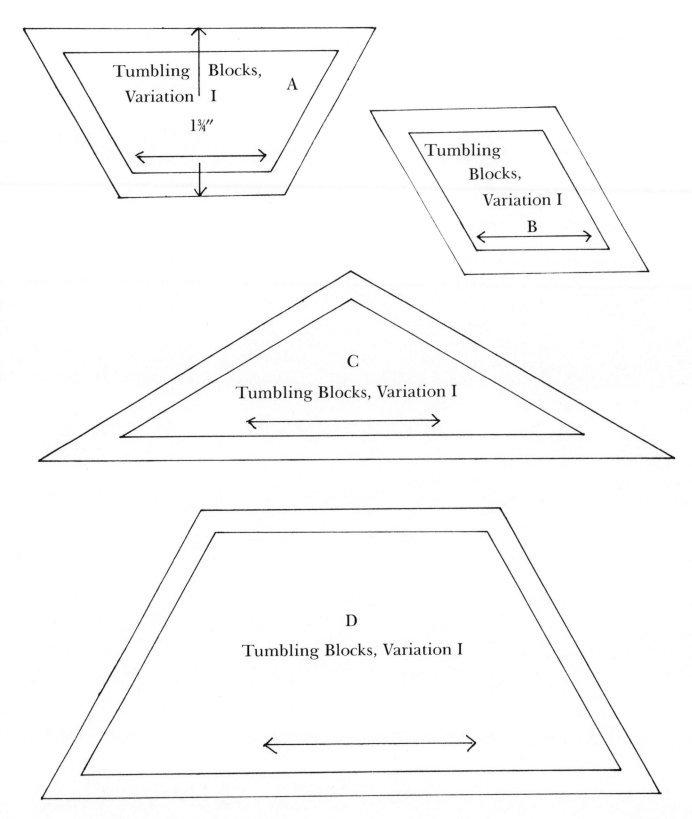

Tumbling | Blocks,
Variation | I
A
1¾″

Tumbling
Blocks,
Variation I
B

C
Tumbling Blocks, Variation I

D
Tumbling Blocks, Variation I

Instructions for this quilt begin on page 29.

Plate 8

Tumbling Blocks, Variation II

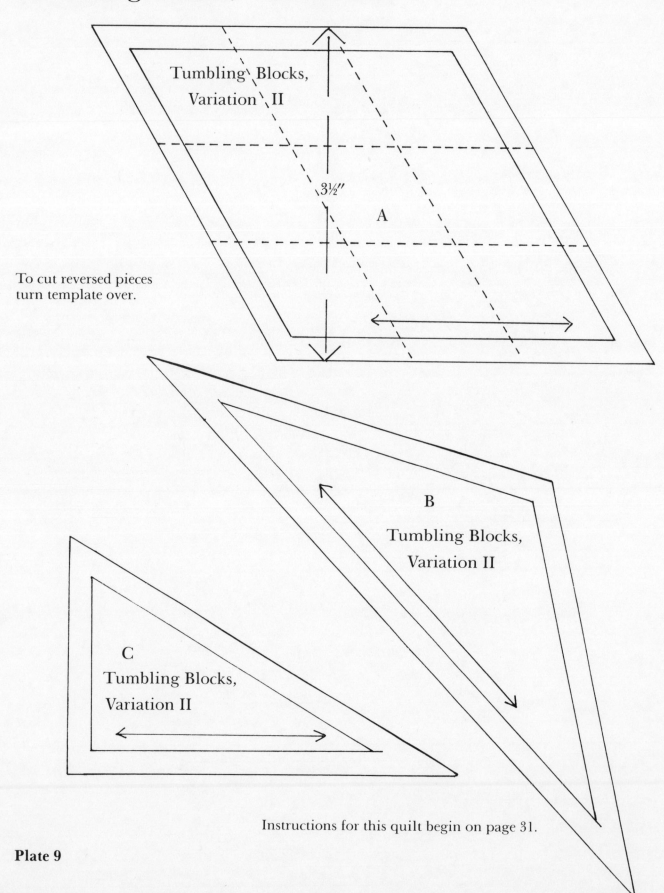

Tumbling Blocks,
Variation II

3½″

A

To cut reversed pieces
turn template over.

B

Tumbling Blocks,
Variation II

C

Tumbling Blocks,
Variation II

Instructions for this quilt begin on page 31.

Plate 9

Tumbling Blocks, Variation III

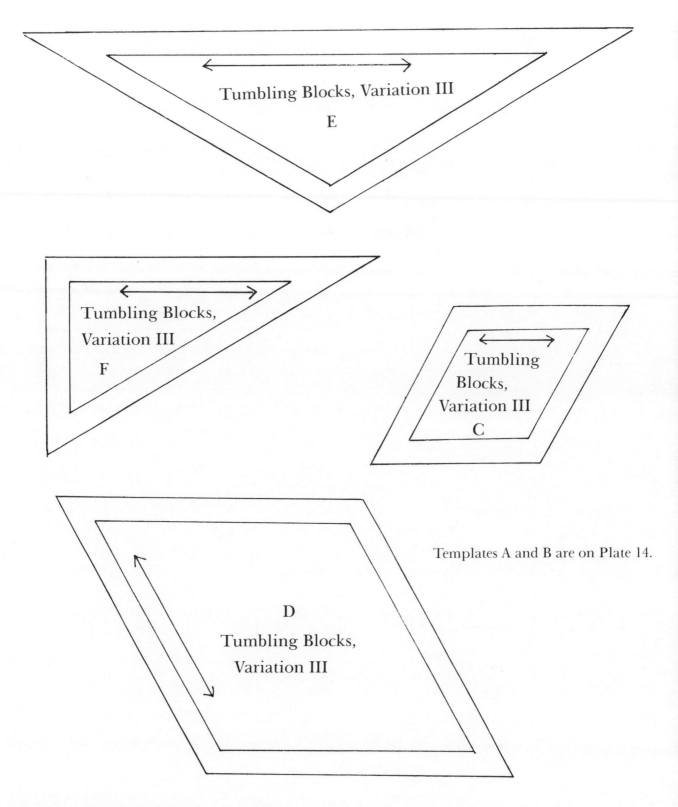

Tumbling Blocks, Variation III

E

Tumbling Blocks,
Variation III

F

Tumbling
Blocks,
Variation III
C

Templates A and B are on Plate 14.

D
Tumbling Blocks,
Variation III

Instructions for this quilt begin on page 33.

Plate 10

Shadow Box, Variation II

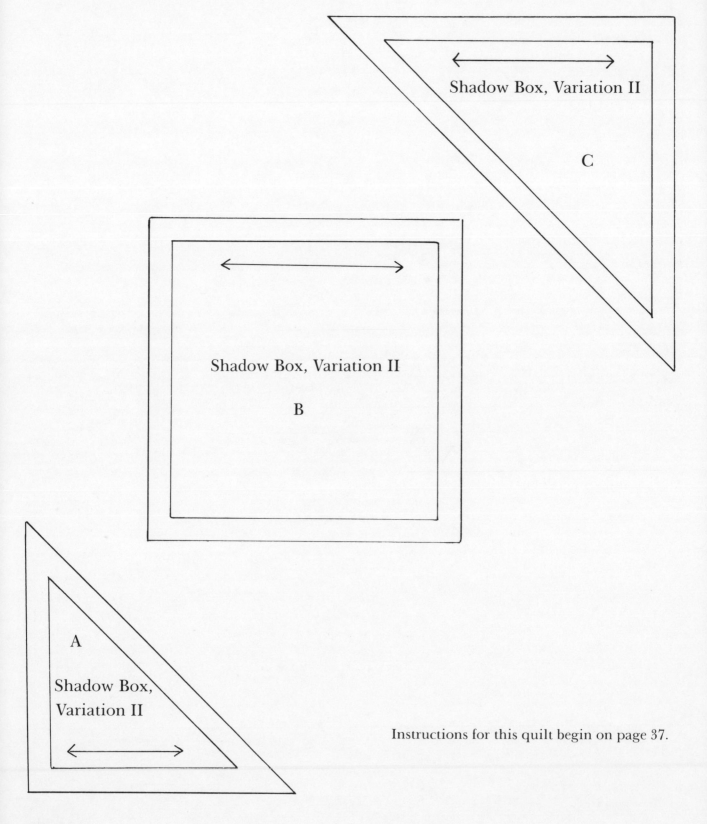

Shadow Box, Variation II

C

Shadow Box, Variation II

B

A

Shadow Box,
Variation II

Instructions for this quilt begin on page 37.

Plate 11

Shadow Box, Variation III

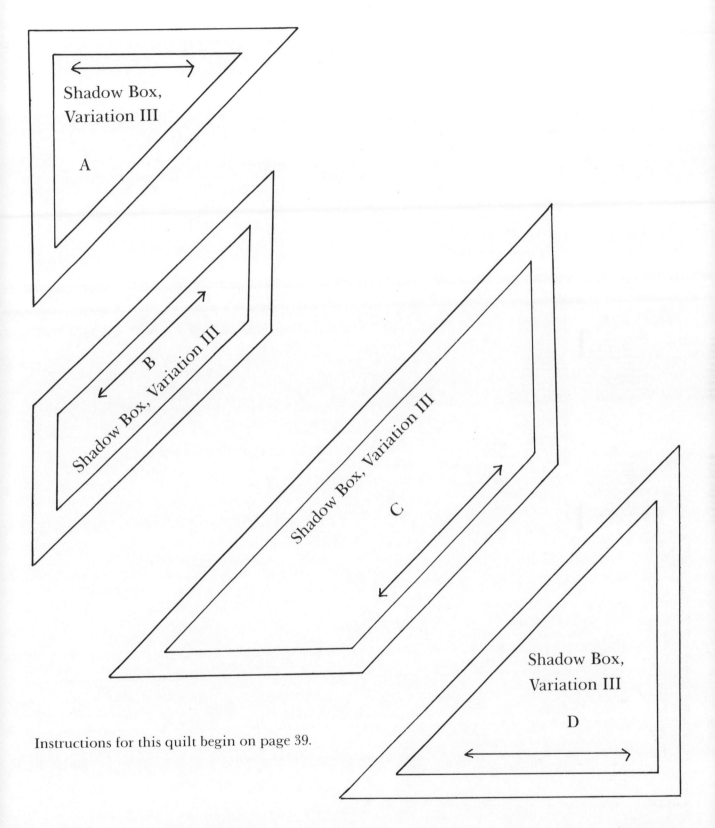

Shadow Box, Variation III

A

Shadow Box, Variation III

B

Shadow Box, Variation III

C

Shadow Box, Variation III

D

Instructions for this quilt begin on page 39.

Plate 12

Three by Three, Variation I

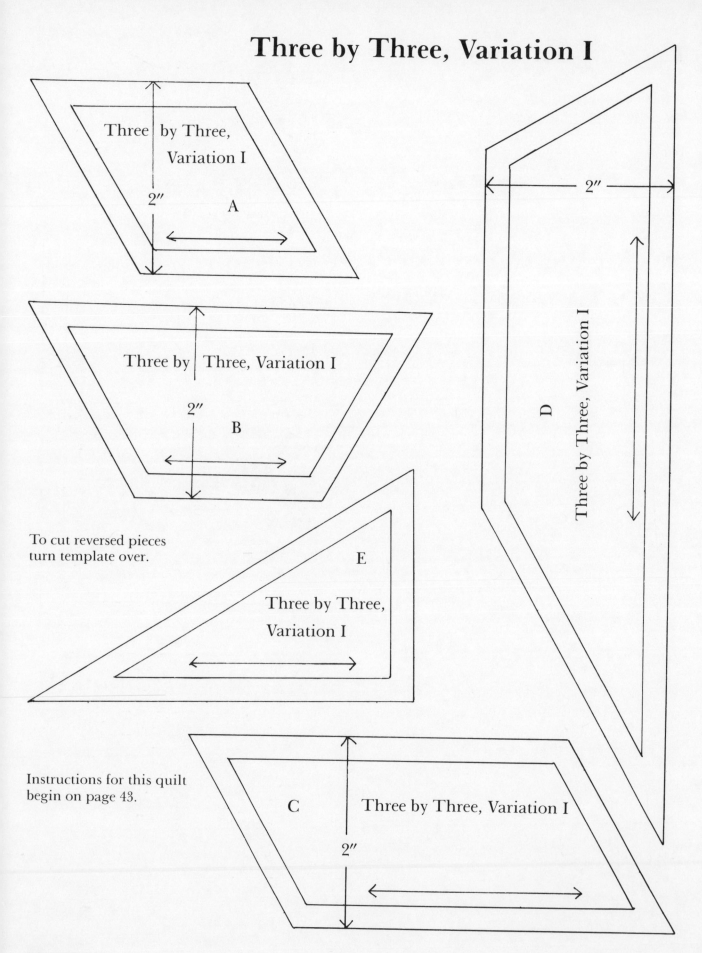

Three by Three, Variation I

2″

A

Three by Three, Variation I

2″

B

To cut reversed pieces turn template over.

E

Three by Three, Variation I

Instructions for this quilt begin on page 43.

C

Three by Three, Variation I

2″

2″

Three by Three, Variation I

D

Plate 13

Three by Three, Variation II

Instructions for this quilt begin on page 45.

Templates A–G are on Plates 15 and 16.

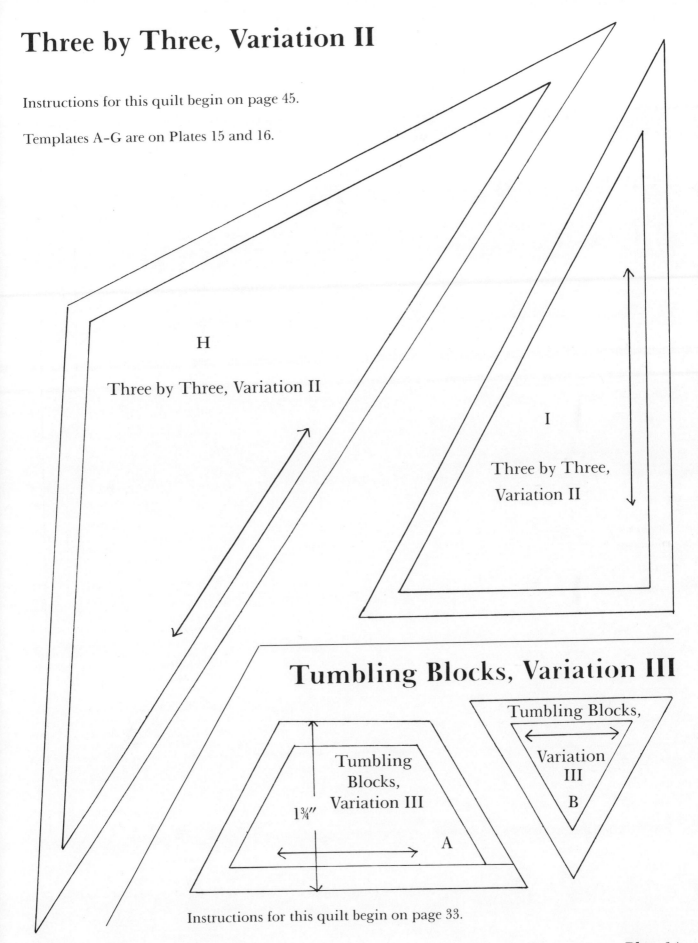

H

Three by Three, Variation II

I

Three by Three,
Variation II

Tumbling Blocks, Variation III

Tumbling Blocks,

Variation
III
B

Tumbling
Blocks,
Variation III

1¾″

A

Instructions for this quilt begin on page 33.

Plate 14

Three by Three, Variation II

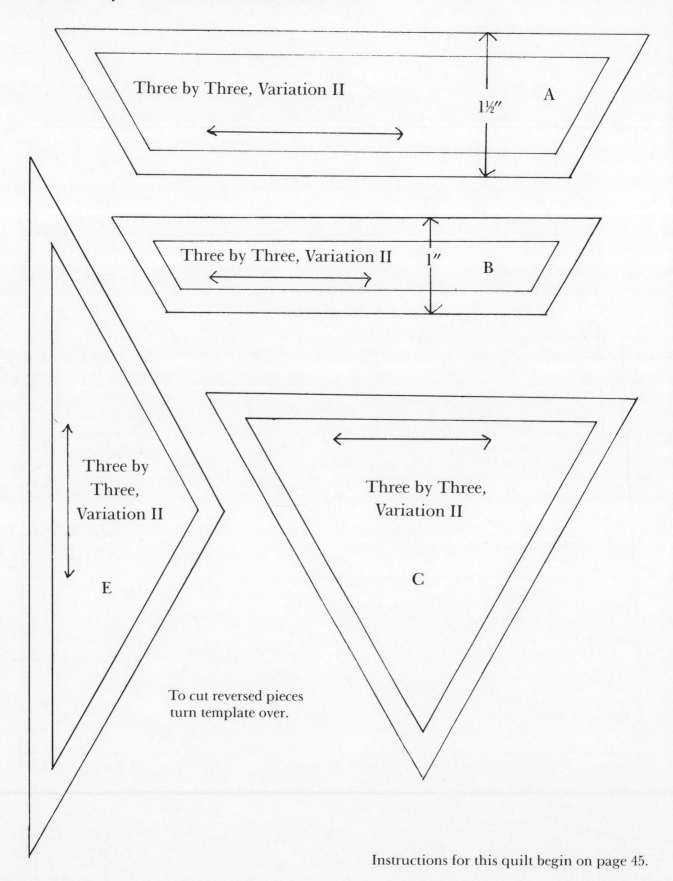

Three by Three, Variation II

1½″

A

Three by Three, Variation II

1″

B

Three by
Three,
Variation II

E

Three by Three,
Variation II

C

To cut reversed pieces
turn template over.

Instructions for this quilt begin on page 45.

Plate 15

Three by Three, Variation II

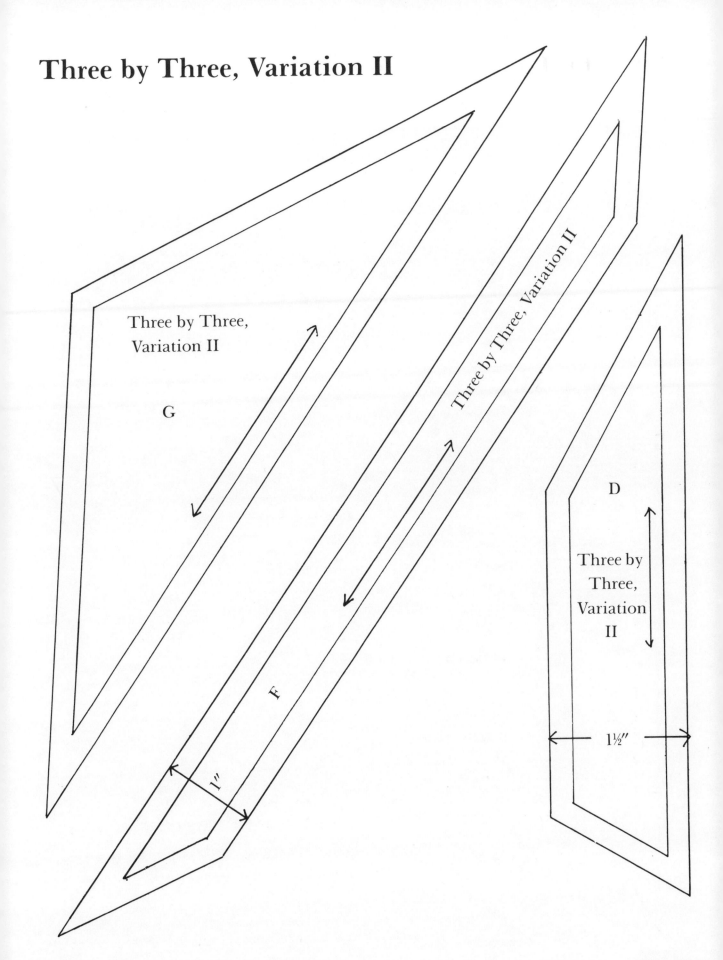

Three by Three,
Variation II

G

Three by Three, Variation II

D

Three by
Three,
Variation
II

F

1½″

1″

Plate 16